DETAILS
MEN'S STYLE MANUAL

DETAILS

MEN'S STYLE MANUAL

THE ULTIMATE GUIDE
FOR MAKING YOUR CLOTHES
WORK FOR YOU

DANIEL PERES
AND THE EDITORS
OF DETAILS

GOTHAM
BOOKS

MELCHER
MEDIA

CONTENTS

Introduction

A few years ago, a story on the front page of the *New York Times* declared, "Daniel Peres is a slob." This was in the first sentence of an article about how it was fashionable for men to wear their shirts untucked, and I was its inspiration. Egos being what they are, the devil in me was thrilled.

In a world of skinny suits and pointy shoes, I was rather content dressing down. I had adopted a uniform of jeans, sweaters, and tattered Chucks—and the occasional button-down shirt, untucked, of course. I even wore a fleece to a Versace fashion show once. In fact, at the men's fashion shows in Milan and Paris, I often looked more like the editor of *Monster Truck Monthly* than *Details*.

While I was convinced I looked, well, devilishly handsome, I have since realized that I was, as the *Times* stated, a slob.

I decided to do something about it. It was time for me to start behaving like a gentleman, and in order to do so, I had to begin dressing like one.

So when it came time to travel to Europe for the next batch of runway shows, I chose to wear a suit and tie every day. Let's just say it wasn't a subtle transformation. "Job interview?" cracked one smart-ass rival editor. "You look so mature," said another, more insulting than complimentary, as if to say, "Hey, why aren't you dressed like a college freshman anymore?" And at least a half-dozen people asked if I was going to a funeral.

I guess, in a way, that's how I used to approach these seasonal fashion exhibitions—with the level of enthusiasm generally reserved for a wake. I had to be there, but I wanted out in the worst way. Well, there's something to be said for osmosis. Years of sitting front row at the collections had changed my interest from faux to genuine.

These designers had finally gotten through to me. I realized the importance of being well dressed. (Don't get me wrong, jeans and sneakers can be very stylish—just not every day.)

This book is here to help you with your own transformation. Whether you've got your act together and simply need some occasional advice, or, like me, you want to give yourself a makeover, this is your guide.

My own sartorial shortcomings notwithstanding, *Details* has always taken fashion seriously. Our editors have consistently presented the right mix of classic and cutting-edge. This book channels much of their collective fashion wisdom into a piece-by-piece evaluation of the male wardrobe. The *Details Men's Style Manual* is your very own fashion editor—the expert you can turn to with any question you may have or any advice you may need.

Style is something extremely personal. No one, especially the editors of *Details*, should tell you how to dress. If you feel confident with your shirt untucked, then by all means don't tuck. I've always maintained that most men already have their own sense of style. But every now and then everyone needs to make some adjustments.

That's exactly what I've done. It's not like I sold my soul to the fashion elite. I've simply changed my tune. And that's the great thing about fashion—there's so much out there to choose from, as long as you're paying attention.

And if, like most men, you're too busy to pay attention on your own, take comfort in the fact that we've done it for you. Everything you need to know is right here. You no longer have an excuse for looking like a slob.

Daniel Peres

RULES OF STYLE

TAKE AN HONEST LOOK IN THE MIRROR AND BE REALISTIC ABOUT WHAT YOU LOOK LIKE.

COMING TO TERMS WITH YOUR BODY TYPE CAN BE LIBERATING. ONCE YOU START WEARING SUITS AND TROUSERS CUT PRECISELY TO FIT YOU, YOU'LL REALIZE THIS. NO MAN LOOKS ELEGANT IN A TOO-TIGHT JACKET OR BAGGY PANTS.

It's okay to wear a uniform.

If you feel most comfortable in a charcoal suit with a pale tie and a pocket square, wear a variation on that outfit five days a week. Powerful men have signature looks.

80% of style is having the right clothes for the occasion.

Dress codes may have relaxed in recent years, but there are still rules. When in doubt, err on the formal side—and if you're going to a business meeting or a cocktail party, you're better off wearing a tie.

Don't try to dress like a movie star unless you are one. Just because Brad Pitt or Johnny Depp can pull it off doesn't mean you can. Go ahead and experiment with trends now and then, but don't wear a porkpie hat because you saw a celebrity do it.

All Together Now.
When you're dressing make sure that you consider the whole look. Your jacket, shirt, tie, pants, and shoes might all be great pieces, but do they work together? Stylish dressing is about creating an overall effect.

CLASSICS
ARE CLASSIC FOR A REASON.
MEN'S STYLE HAS CHANGED LITTLE OVER THE PAST ONE HUNDRED YEARS. YOU SHOULDN'T BE THE PERSON WHO TRIES TO BREAK THE MOLD. WHEN IN DOUBT, ASK YOURSELF, "WHAT WOULD CARY GRANT DO?"

Be inquisitive.
If a friend is looking particularly sharp go ahead and find out where he buys his threads. Chances are his answer will broaden your horizons.

Don't try too hard.
Strive for being stylish rather than fashionable and remember that the most important person to dress for is you.

CLASSICS YOU SHOULD ALREADY OWN

☐ AN OVERCOAT THAT COMPLEMENTS CUSTOM SUITS AND MAKES JEANS LOOK ELEGANT

☐ A SINGLE-BREASTED NAVY BLUE SUIT AND A GRAY SUIT, BOTH IN A MEDIUM WEIGHT THAT YOU CAN WEAR YEAR-ROUND

☐ A NAVY BLAZER

☐ TWO PAIRS OF GOOD SHOES— ONE BLACK, THE OTHER DARK BROWN

X2

 A SLIM
DARK-
COLORED
TIE

X2

☐
TWO WHITE
SHIRTS

☐
ONE BLUE
SHIRT

☐
TWO POLO
SHIRTS

☐
A SIMPLE
BLACK BELT

☐
A PAIR OF BASIC
STRAIGHT-LEG
BLUE JEANS

☐
SEVERAL PAIRS
OF BLACK COTTON
SOCKS

SHIRTS

CHAPTER 1

Once upon a time, the average working guy's closet contained maybe a dozen off-the-rack button-down shirts—all in blue or white. But in the last decade—with mostly positive results—men have become braver, savvier, and more discerning. Bright colors, stripes, and prints have infiltrated their wardrobes. Shirts with spread collars and French cuffs are rubbing shoulders with all-American Brooks Brothers models. As this sartorial renaissance unfolds, men are also developing an appreciation for the most crucial part of shirt selection: fit. No matter how much a button-down shirt costs, if it isn't cut precisely to fit the wearer's body, it's a liability—which means the shirtmakers on Savile Row who once seemed destined to become dinosaurs now seem progressive. So seize the moment and make some room in your closet. Start with the perfect white shirt—preferably a simple, custom-made one—and go from there.

SHIRT BASICS

① THE PLAIN CUFF

Shirts that don't require cuff links should have one button at the cuff and a small "chisel" where the heel of your hand cocks back. If you want a slightly more formal style—but still no links—wear a shirt with barrel cuffs, which have two buttons and no chisel.

② THE FRENCH CUFF

Some unenlightened dressers think French cuffs are stuffy. They're not. You can wear a shirt with cuffs that fasten with links, not buttons, every day—even with jeans and a blazer. Just be sure to calibrate the formality of the hardware—silk knots are better for daytime than 14-karat gold—and never leave the cuffs unfolded and trailing out your sleeve, or you'll look like the fourth tenor.

③ THE COLLAR

A collar shape—whether it's spread, long point, or another style (see page 24)—that flatters your face, your build, and your personal aesthetic is crucial. It can be the best argument for having your shirts custom-made.

④ THE BUTTONS

The quality of the buttons will clue you in to the quality of the shirt. A well-made one should have thick, triple-stacked, mother-of-pearl buttons—not flimsy plastic disks that crack in half on the first trip to the dry cleaner. It should also have a gauntlet button—that's the one between the wrist and the elbow that allows you to roll your sleeves up neatly.

⑤ THE FABRIC

Like sheets, shirts come in thread counts from low to luxuriously high. Some companies make shirts with thread counts as high as 180. But the truth is, you're better off with good, serviceable cotton. Extremely high grades may be silkier, but they wear out faster and cost more. There are many weaves for shirts from the casual oxford and chambray to the smooth pima and Sea Island.

CUFF LINKS? GO TO PAGE 240

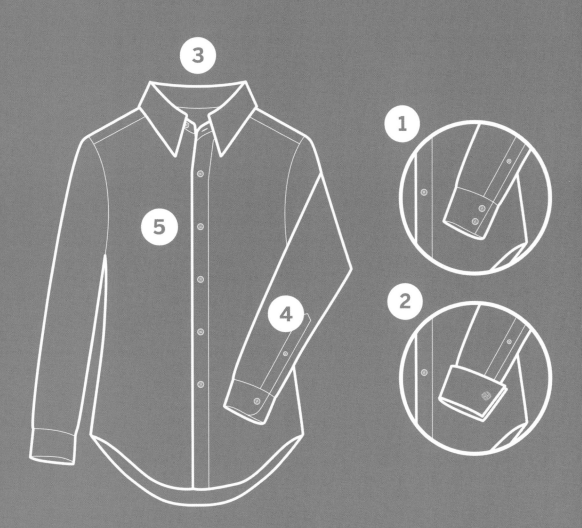

THE PERFECT SHIRT

Men who take their clothes seriously have their white shirts custom-made. There's a reason for that. The right shirt is the cornerstone of a man's wardrobe. It's the pristine anchor for a formal suit and the crisp complement to a blazer and jeans. If you can, retrace the steps of style icons like J.F.K., Gianni Agnelli, and Tom Wolfe and make a pilgrimage to one of the classic shirtmakers lining Jermyn Street in London, like Turnbull & Asser, Alexander Kabbaz in New York, or Charvet in Paris (if you can't find the perfect white shirt at Charvet, it can't be found). Select the style you want, keep the embellishments to a minimum—a custom-made white shirt doesn't need pockets and monograms—and order more than one. When you're scanning your closet at the crack of dawn for a fast way to look sharp, you'll be thankful.

OPTIONS

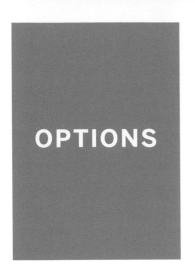

BLUE

Everything goes with a blue shirt. When white seems too stark, sub in one in any shade—from powdery to bright.

CHECKS

There's no better way to breathe life into a gray suit than with a gingham shirt—even a black-and-white one does the job.

STRIPED OXFORD

The striped oxford is an all-American classic. You can pair it with jeans or khakis—tie optional—and feel free to roll up the sleeves.

CONTRAST COLLAR

The contrast collar isn't just for bankers. Worn with a dark suit, the distinguished shirt works for any dressed-up event.

MILITARY

Shirts with military detailing have a structured elegance that make them slightly more dressy than the average button-down. Wear one out to dinner, without a tie.

VARIEGATED STRIPES

This suave, Italian-style pattern is better suited for evenings out than boardroom meetings. Just keep the number of undone buttons to a minimum.

GRAY

The gray shirt is an underrated alternative to blue and white. In fact, a dove-colored one is an even better complement to navy suits.

PLAID

The associations with grunge and golf have been vanquished. The new breed of plaid shirt looks well with suits and ties or just tucked into trousers.

PENCIL STRIPES

The pencil-stripe shirt adds dimension to a suit-and-tie without overwhelming it. Just make sure the stripes are slender and the colors are coordinated.

BAND COLLAR

The band-collar shirt had a bad moment during the days of *Miami Vice*. It's now made a comeback as a worthy alternative to the oxford.

FLORAL PRINT

It takes moxie to pull off a flower-print shirt. The very confident can wear oversize, brightly colored styles; the rest of us should go for something more understated.

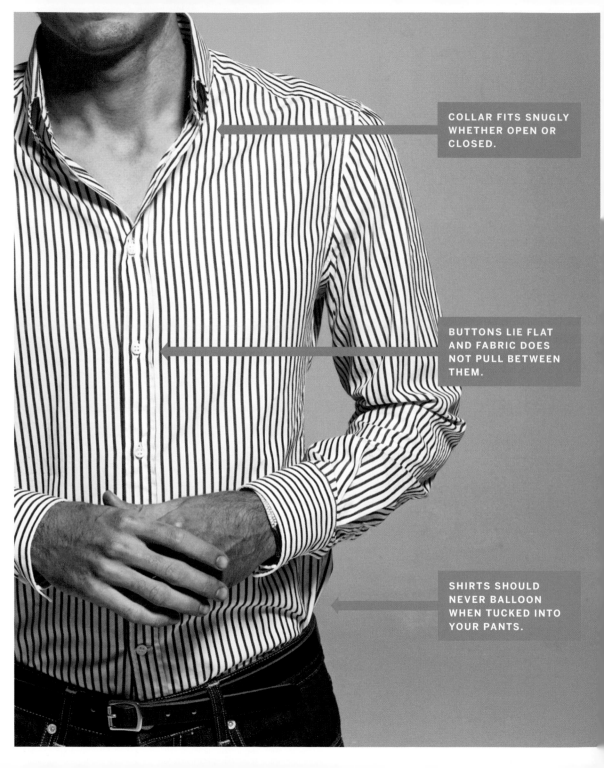

COLLAR FITS SNUGLY WHETHER OPEN OR CLOSED.

BUTTONS LIE FLAT AND FABRIC DOES NOT PULL BETWEEN THEM.

SHIRTS SHOULD NEVER BALLOON WHEN TUCKED INTO YOUR PANTS.

THE PERFECT FIT

No matter what you paid for it—or how trim your torso—if your shirt doesn't fit properly, you're going to look like a schlump. Most men wear theirs a full half size too big. And a blousy, billowy shirt is just as unflattering as a skin-tight one. And while you may have your measurements memorized, the numbers don't always add up—no two manufacturers' shirts fit exactly alike. Try a shirt on before you buy it, take an honest look at yourself in the mirror, and follow these guidelines for honing in on the perfect fit:

THE TORSO

There's a lot of middle ground between too loose and too tight. Find it. The shirt should be snug in the chest, but not so snug that the fabric pulls between the buttons.

THE BACK

Beefier guys should get a shirt with box pleats in the back—two folds between the shoulder blades—for a little more room, without extra volume. Those with slimmer builds should opt for fitted styles that contour down toward the waist. Either way, the seams of the shirt should lie on the curve of your deltoids (those are the muscles right behind your shoulders—the ones you'd work if you did push-ups).

THE WAIST

Sit down while you're wearing the shirt. It should skim your waist but leave just enough room to give when you're seated (and full).

THE NECK

The golden rule here hasn't changed: You should be able to comfortably fit two fingers in between your neck and the collar of the shirt when it's buttoned.

THE SLEEVES

The cuffs of the shirt should fall in the crook between the base of your thumb and your wrist.

THE TAILS

The tails should be long enough to lie under your rear end when you're seated. That will prevent the shirt from riding up or coming untucked. It will also give you better posture.

 In 1905, to help with flagging sales, the **Arrow Collar Man** debuted in Arrow Collar Company's advertising campaigns. Sales of shirts soared, and **by 1920 the imaginary Arrow Collar Man was receiving more fan mail than Rudolph Valentino.**

Collars

REGULAR
The classic multitasking shirt for every occasion. Wear with a tie to work and remove the tie for evening cocktails.

SPREAD
This British classic is unequivocally formal. It calls for a properly knotted tie—though a Windsor isn't mandatory—and a well-cut suit.

BUTTON-DOWN
This old-school collar evokes prep school. Dress it up with a tie or embrace its casual roots and wear it without one.

TAB
The business-like tab collar does double duty, pulling the collar flat around the neck and propping your tie up so it stands at attention.

LONG POINT
Long-point collars have a slightly dramatic effect. The tie is optional and a button or two can be undone (see Tom Ford's signature look).

Fit Tips

TIP (1)

A collar should balance the shape of your face. Wide collars like spreads complement long, narrow faces (John Kerry), and pointed collars look best with round ones (Jack Black). A too-tight collar, of course, flatters no one.

TIP (2)

Athletic guys should look for fitted shirts that contour down; bigger builds will want to look for a box pleat.

MEASURE UP: THE THREE TROUBLE SPOTS WITH SHIRTS ARE AT THE NECK, THE SLEEVE, AND IN THE WAIST. NECKS AND ARMS ARE A SIMPLE MATTER OF GETTING THE RIGHT MEASUREMENTS.

DRESS UP, DRESS DOWN

How to wear one white shirt for four different occasions.

Ⓐ THE PRESENTATION
Let your clothes make a power point without distracting them from your Power Point. The white shirt creates great contrast with a sharp black suit.

Ⓑ DINNER DATE AT THE DINER
Dark jeans and the same white shirt with a great pair of brown shoes are dressy enough without being too uptight to have fun.

WINTER WINDOW SHOPPING
A flash of white under layers of gray wool wakes the whole ensemble up.

SUNDAY DRIVE
Stop in to see the in-laws then swing by the bar to catch the game. The white shirt tones the gray down without making it too washed out.

HOW TO PULL OFF

The Print Shirt

It's possible to wear a printed shirt without looking like Fred Schneider of the B-52s—or worse, being mistaken for one of the martini-swilling prowlers at VIP clubs. In truth, a patterned shirt—multicolored stripes and subtle abstract or floral prints—shouldn't be reserved for Friday nights. You can wear a slim-fitting one with tailored trousers to cocktail hour or with jeans to Sunday brunch. Paired with a solid-colored suit and tie, a brightly printed shirt can even go to the office. Just let the playfulness of the material speak for itself and keep the shirt neatly tucked into your pants, your hair gel-free, and no more than two buttons at the neck undone.

BEGINNER
If you'd rather the shirt not turn heads, look for a small, repeated pattern in just two colors, like checks or slim stripes.

INTERMEDIATE
So long as it's balanced out with solid-colored trousers, a vivid printed shirt will look sophisticated, not garish. Try one in a bright color-block or multicolored abstract print.

ADVANCED
Yes, you can wear a shirt in a bright, oversize floral or abstract print to the office. In fact, any complicated, eye-catching pattern can be matched with a solid suit and tie—you just have to wear it with pride.

DON'TS

DON'T WEAR DENIM SHIRTS
If you own cattle, ignore this warning. Everyone else should stay away from denim shirts, especially with jeans. You think you look like the Marlboro Man, but be honest, you don't.

DON'T OVERPOWER YOURSELF
Calling too much attention to one part of your shirt—let alone to yourself—is always a risk. Remember that you're wearing a shirt, not a neon sign.

DON'T UNBUTTON YOUR SHIRT TOO FAR
Two words for you: Tom Jones. Wear your shirts unbuttoned to the navel and they'll be thinking "What's New Pussycat?" Who needs that?

HOW TO BUY

CUSTOM-MADE

IF YOU'RE BUYING CUSTOM-MADE, THE TAILOR WILL DO MOST OF THE WORK FOR YOU, AND YOUR OPTIONS FOR CUT AND MATERIAL ARE LIMITLESS. BUT KNOW THIS: THE PATTERN YOU CHOOSE WILL AFFECT YOUR COLLAR AND CUFF CHOICES, AND VICE VERSA. A FORMAL SHIRT STYLE WITH TOO CASUAL A PATTERN OR FABRIC WON'T WORK. BUT THE BEAUTY OF BESPOKE IS THAT COUNSEL COMES WITH THE SERVICE.

KNOW YOUR MEASUREMENTS

A salesman at any good store—whether you're having your shirt custom-made or not—should be adept at taking them. And have them retaken at least once a year—things change.

Don't just pick out the shirts you like—have a solid rotation in mind.

If you've got a closetful of suits and jackets in pinstripes and plaids, make sure you have a good supply of solid-colored shirts. If you tend toward plain navy and gray suits, stock up on shirts in bright stripes and checks. Whatever your preference, work several perfectly cut white shirts into the mix.

THREE DEGREES OF THE WELL-DRESSED MAN

Sophisticated

George Clooney

Frank Sinatra

Cary Grant   J.F.K.

Anderson Cooper

Leonardo DiCaprio   Barack Obama

Clive Owen

Matt Lauer

Tom Ford   Hugh Grant

Warren Beatty

Tiger Woods   Richard Gere

Terrence Howard

Jake Gyllenhaal

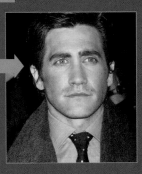

Oscar de la Renta

Trendy

Andy Warhol   Truman Capote

David Beckham   Ashton Kutcher

Justin Timberlake

André 3000

Pharrell Williams

Karl Lagerfeld   Pete Doherty

Jude Law

Kanye West

Orlando Bloom

David Bowie   Colin Farrell

Johnny Depp

Brad Pitt   Bono

Hedi Slimane

Laid-back/Relaxed

Bruce Springsteen

James Dean   Sean Penn

Robert Redford

Matt Damon   Ewan McGregor

Harrison Ford   Ethan Hawke

Viggo Mortensen

Owen Wilson

Matthew McConaughey

Ben Affleck   Tom Brady

Ryan Phillippe

Marc Jacobs   Keanu Reeves

Josh Hartnett

PANTS

CHAPTER 2

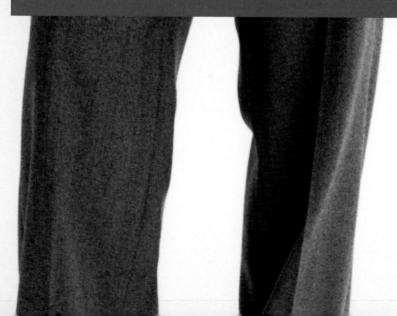

You may think that choosing a pair of pants is simple enough. That's your mistake right there. Pants are a style minefield. They can be too long, too short, too baggy, and even too stonewashed. Choose the wrong pair and you could end up looking like MC Hammer. To get them right ask yourself two simple questions: First, do they fit? Second, do they suit your taste? Never try to go "freestyle" with pants. They're not the item in your wardrobe with which to demonstrate your flair and virtuosity. A final word of advice: No man has ever successfully pulled off capri pants. Do not attempt to be the first.

PANTS BASICS

① THE WAIST

A question: Where's your waist? If you're stumped, chances are you don't really know your waist size either. That means your pants don't fit. To remedy this, place a tape measure around your midsection just above your hipbone. Commit the number to memory.

② THE RISE

The rise is the length of the fly, or the section from the crotch to your waistband. A long rise gives you a high waist. A short rise puts you in hip-huggers. A really short rise makes you a member of Fall Out Boy.

③ THE INSEAM

Running vertically from the crotch to the cuff, the inseam gives you the length of your leg. It's the second number in your jeans formula (as in 34 waist, 32 inseam). Unless you have long arms and phenomenal flexibility, you might need someone else to measure this for you.

④ THE BELT LOOPS

Not all pants have belt loops, but if they do make use of them. They're not there for decoration.

⑤ THE POCKETS

Cell phone, keys, iPod...The modern man has plenty to lug around with him. That is no excuse for overloading your pockets and ruining the contour of your pants. There are a wide variety of side pockets: on the seam, diagonal jets, slanted, depending on the formality of the pant. At the back you can choose buttoned or open pockets, one (on the right side) or two. Whatever you decide, lose the bulging wallet.

⑥ THE CUFFS

After having a moment in the eighties, cuffs are more the exception than the rule, except for those jean connoisseurs who like to show off their shuttle-loom-spun Japanese denim. With trousers, if you do choose cuffs, be sure the tailor makes them in proportion to your body size. Too big and you'll look like an extra from *The Untouchables*.

⑦ THE FABRIC

More than any other item of clothing, your trousers take a pounding. From your morning commute to hours sitting on a bar stool listening to Brian from sales, your pants' arduous routine requires that they be durable. They also have to be appropriate for the season. If you're playing golf at lunchtime in August you might want to leave your tweed pair at home.

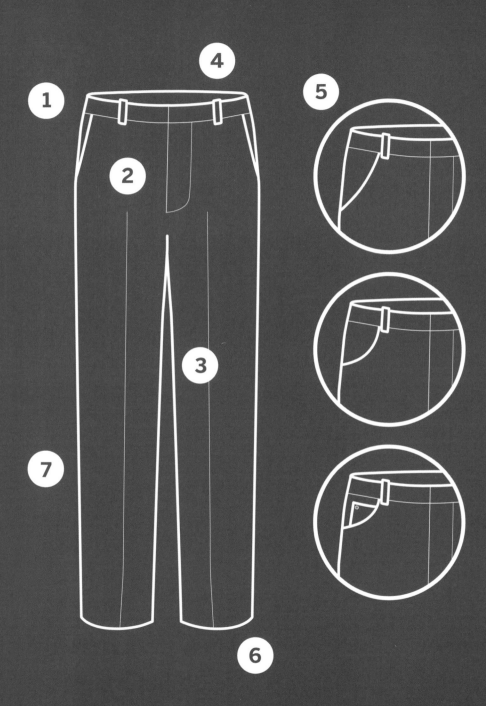

THE PERFECT PANTS

Gray is the ultimate neutral color—the Switzerland of the sartorial palette—which makes it an excellent choice if you want pants that are versatile enough to wear with almost anything. The pearly hue complements bold colors, so feel free to get creative with your choice of shirt—blue, red, black, brown, and even pastel shades are all fair game.

As for whether the perfect gray trousers should be pleated or flat-front, that's up to you. The truth is that pleats are there to help the pant drape better. Our advice? Go flat-fronted. It's a more modern look and almost always more flattering. One other thing: if you're wondering how your cell phone will look clipped to these pants, you should stop reading this book right now.

OPTIONS

KHAKI

Its origins in the British military make khaki's strengths clear: the fabric is tough, and it is suitable for both office and urban combat. Opt for modern cuts for pants—slim, flat-fronted—that many retailers have made available over the past few years.

BLACK

This is your alternative to navy blue. Just don't wear pants in the somber color with a white shirt— you'll end up being asked what the entrée special is.

NAVY CHINO

These pants can do double-duty as dressy weekend attire or casual work wear. Pair them with a slim-fitting white oxford shirt.

PLEATED

Pants with pleats hang better. They give the crease more room to fall and make your legs look longer. But no pair of pants needs more than two pleats.

PINSTRIPE

Match a pair of pinstripe trousers—the lines should be pencil thin—with a pressed collared shirt and you have a fail-safe dinner-party uniform.

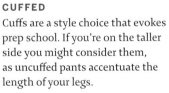

LINEN

If you ever need to sleep in your pants, make sure they're linen. The fabric, which is made from flax, looks great rumpled: It also absorbs moisture, and will keep you cool on the hottest of days.

CUFFED

Cuffs are a style choice that evokes prep school. If you're on the taller side you might consider them, as uncuffed pants accentuate the length of your legs.

TWEED

The Scottish textile has lost its fuddy-duddy image and is now a fixture in many designer collections. And whether it's in the form of checks, herringbone, or twill, tweed is a great choice for pants, as it's Mike Tyson tough.

CARGO

Both high-end designers and mainstream fashion retailers made a mint off cargo pants during the dress-down nineties. And as long as you don't stuff the pockets, the military-inspired pants are still a great alternative to jeans and khakis—on weekends only.

WOOL FLANNEL

Another durable choice, flannel's warmth and softness are surely the qualities that made it such a big hit with L.A. gang bangers a decade ago. Pants cut from the cloth are a good choice even if your name doesn't have the word *Dogg* in it.

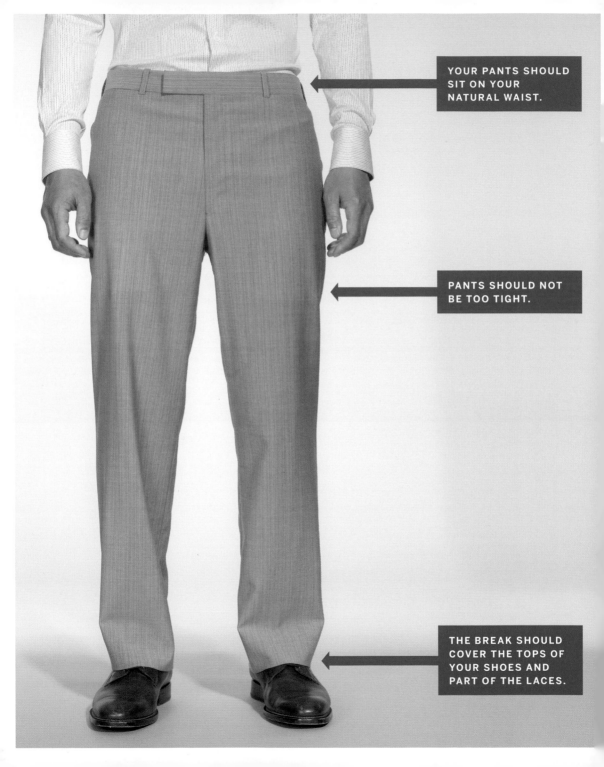

YOUR PANTS SHOULD SIT ON YOUR NATURAL WAIST.

PANTS SHOULD NOT BE TOO TIGHT.

THE BREAK SHOULD COVER THE TOPS OF YOUR SHOES AND PART OF THE LACES.

THE PERFECT FIT

OVERALL

Your pants should be snug around your waist, but not too tight, the hem should touch your shoe, but not cover it, and the shape of the pant should be appropriate for your frame.

THE NATURAL WAIST

It's just below your belly button. If your pants sit any higher, you'll officially be wearing "Dad pants."

THE JEANS WAIST

Jeans are meant to be worn a bit lower and closer to the hips than other pants. Think old Levi's and Toughskins. But no matter how much juice you think you have on the streets, leave the low-rider pants to the B-boys.

THE HEM

One of the keys to good style is knowing what suits you. And part of this is coming to terms with what the good Lord has (or hasn't) endowed you with. If you're tall, then you should consider cuffing your pants. If you're short, lose the cuffs (and the Cuban heels, for that matter).

THE BREAK

The break is where your pants touch your shoes. The lower the break, the deeper the horizontal crease that sits on your shoe. The three different types are: medium (your pants will fall midway between the top of your shoe and the top of the sole), full (which drapes fabric over the shoe top and sweeps it back to a quarter inch above the floor in the back), and short (pants are worn high on the leg with a quarter inch of swing between the bottoms and the top of the shoe.) Currently, the fashion cognoscenti and designers such as Thom Browne favor the short break. When in doubt, go for a medium break—it's the classic choice.

PLEATS VS. NO PLEATS

Let's make this real simple: Unless you're built like John Goodman or you see yourself as a middle-management "road warrior," then there is no reason to wear pants with multiple pleats. In some cases, however, well-placed pleats, which help pants drape better and make legs look longer, can be flattering.

! **One sheep** yields about five pounds of wool, enough for **a couple of pairs of pants.**

The Hem

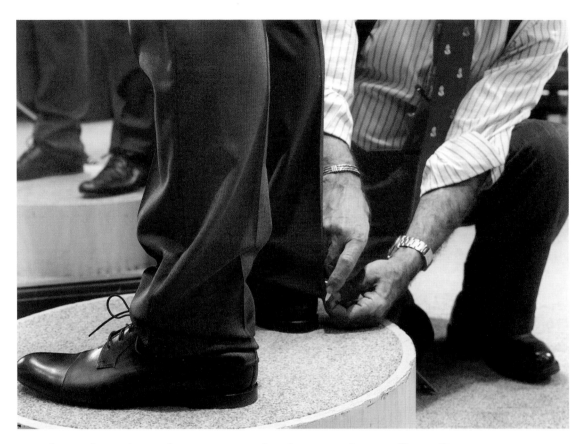

One hem doesn't work on every pair of pants. If you tell a tailor
to make your jeans the same length as your pleated trousers,
you could wind up looking like Pee-Wee Herman. Regardless of
what you're having shortened, be sure to bring the appropriate
shoes and let your pants sit where they're comfortable.

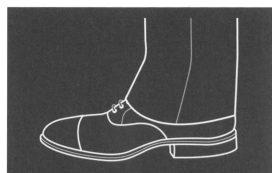

THE STRAIGHT HEM

The proper hem for flat-front trousers is straight—not a cuff. The bottom of your pants should stop an inch above the sole of your shoe, which creates a small break (a fold in the crease in the front of the pants) at the ankle.

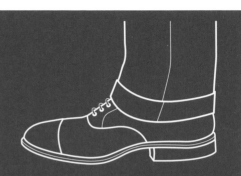

THE CUFF

Pleated pants looks best with a cuff because it balances out the billowy fabric at the waist. The cuff should be an inch and a half wide, and the length and the break the same as with a straight hem.

THE CROP

A short hem, one that exposes about an inch of ankle, works on just about any narrow-cut pants—flat-front or pleated, wool or cotton. A cuff is optional, but if you opt for one, it should be wider than the standard inch and a half, but no more than two and a quarter inches (that's high-water territory).

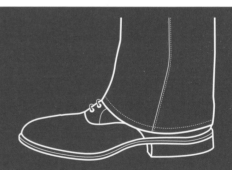

THE JEANS

Have your jeans cut slightly longer than your tailored pants; they should end a half an inch above the sole of your sneakers (if they're straight-leg, the hem can go all the way to the floor). And make sure the tailor stitches the original hem of the jeans back on after he shortens them so the chop job is imperceptible.

Shorts and Swimwear

SHORTS

Shorts should be worn with caution. By all means, mow the lawn in shorts, lounge by the pool in them, even stroll through your local farmers' market displaying your legs to the world. Do not, however, enter your boss's office for your next performance appraisal wearing shorts or go on a date wearing them unless you're a professional surfer. And avoid going to a restaurant without covering your legs unless you're in the drive-thru lane. If it's that hot out, wear summer-weight pants.

If shorts *are* appropriate for the occasion, choose a style that is in proportion to your body and flatters your best features. Got legs Floyd Landis would envy? Then go for the shorter—mid-thigh—shorts. Got chicken legs? Get a knee-length pair that are more like abbreviated pants.

DENIM SHORTS

SWIMWEAR

Unlike our European friends, who have a fondness for bathing suits that resemble briefs, American men are most comfortable with what are essentially shorts made from quick-drying fabric. Don't ignore the fit of your trunks. Try them on to figure out if they're appropriate for your body shape. The leaner you are, the more fitted you can go. If you have a fuller figure, a more generous bathing suit will help to balance things out.

RUNNING SHORTS

CARGO SHORTS

TROUSER SHORTS

ELASTIC-WAIST SWIM TRUNKS

CLASSIC-CUT SWIM TRUNKS

DRESS UP, DRESS DOWN

How to wear one pair of gray pants for four different occasions.

(A) FRIDAY BUSINESS MEETING
Adding a tie tells them you take their business seriously; the sport jacket and cotton pants say that you're all friends.

(B) CORPORATE RETREAT
Paired with a sweater and a collared shirt, the gray pants lend gravitas without making you seem grave.

C POKER ROOM AT THE BELLAGIO

Matching the pants with a tie and collared button-down shirt shows your tablemates that you've got big plans for after you take their money.

D TO THE BALLPARK

Distinguished gray trousers become game-worthy with a polo shirt and a casual jacket.

HOW TO PULL OFF

White Pants

White pants are something of a statement and, for this reason, they can be intimidating to some men. Pull them off by remembering that it's all about balance: Pair them with the right items, and you'll be more Jay Gatsby in West Egg than the Skipper on *Gilligan's Island*.

BEGINNER

White jeans are the best place to start. Contrast them with some color—a bright polo shirt, for instance—and a pair of loafers for an effortlessly cool look straight from the Côte d'Azur. (Just keep the knitwear off your shoulders.)

INTERMEDIATE

Once you've mastered the jeans, move on to white or cream-colored linen pants. Nothing keeps you cooler during the summer months. Wear a contrasting shirt in a subtle color—black or navy are good—and a pair of dark suede shoes.

ADVANCED

For those willing to turn up the summer style stakes to 11, white pants and a blue blazer (or if you have a lot of confidence, a white pinstripe suit) are the height of summer elegance. Again, make sure you wear a contrasting shirt, and pair the outfit with black oxford shoes and a braided belt for full-on Nantucket sophistication.

DON'TS

DON'T DO PLAID
Unless you're named Jock or
are going to a costume party as
Braveheart.

DON'T WEAR SUSPENDERS
You're not Gordon Gekko and you
might end up looking like an extra
from Ringling Bros.

DON'T WEAR PANTS
THAT ARE TOO TIGHT
No one's impressed by a bulge.

HOW TO BUY

CHANCES ARE YOU DON'T HAVE ENOUGH PANTS.

SURE, YOU'VE GOT SOME SUITS AND SOME JEANS. YOU MIGHT HAVE A PAIR OF KHAKIS. BUT YOU'VE GOT TO GO OUT AND GET SOME GOOD PANTS.

TIGHT VS. BAGGY

Get your numbers right: waist and inseam are a good start. But don't just go by the numbers, try the pants on. There's a good chance you're buying your pants a little too tight. They're not jeans, you know. Now check that they don't pull across your rear and that you've got room in the legs and the crotch. It may sound basic, but if you grew up in nothing but jeans you're going to think that's the way pants should fit—too tight. When you've got all that figured out, you can go to a tailor and sweat your way through the tough details like cuffs and the break.

Proper alterations can make a good pair of pants into a great one.

Length is the obvious place a tailor can work his magic. You will have to decide about cuffs and breaks, but remember to take into account the weight of the cloth and the way you plan to wear your shoes. Another way a tailor can save the day is in the seat and crotch. Get these dimensions right—lots of guys need a little more room there—and your pants are going to be as comfortable as a second skin. Beware of trying to take the waist in too much. More than an inch and you should be buying a different pair of pants. Also, ask the tailor to leave the extra fabric in the seams. You never know when you might need to go in the other direction.

RULES
OF STYLE

Giorgio
Armani

1 Clothing is the outward expression of the inner person. It's important to dress in a way that sends the right message but also looks effortless and natural. Wearing clothing that is inappropriate to your inner character is the biggest mistake a man can make in terms of fashion.

2 An air of mystery is a very sensual thing. I don't believe that women need to show a lot of skin to be sexy—why reveal to the entire world what is yet to be unwrapped?

3 Sexy is not a matter of age; it's a matter of attitude. Look at Richard Gere and Annette Bening. Have they ever looked more beautiful than they do today? Being an Italian man of a certain age, I would argue that sexiness increases as you get older. There is something very attractive about experience.

4 If you're a man lost for style, find a male role model. Who do you identify with? Are you a Brad Pitt kind of guy? Or do you see yourself more as a Derek Jeter? And go shopping. Men are so afraid of this; it makes no sense.

5 Growing up in Milan, I went to the cinema constantly and was captivated by the impossibly glamorous men that I saw. Movie stars like Clark Gable, James Dean, and Cary Grant. Cary Grant just looks amazing in a suit—even when he's being chased by a crop duster through a field of corn. You can learn how to be smooth by watching a man like that.

6 I believe in adventure in clothing but I do not believe in spandex superhero costumes.

7 Always take the advice of a woman over that of a man. *Always.* Men tend to regard your outfits solely in terms of whether they'd wear them themselves, but women have an uncanny ability to distance themselves from things like this.

8 My taste in music has always been eclectic. I love Cole Porter, and I love 50 Cent. If I need to put myself in a good mood, I go straight for OutKast. I believe the one thing that everybody needs to do before they're through is see U2 live.

9 There is a French phrase, *nostalgie de la boue*. It means to romanticize low culture—literally, "nostalgia for mud." That is probably what is going on with Hollywood style these days. Young people always want to dress down. I say, why not? Experiment now, because as you grow older, you'll become more set in style, and things will maybe become a bit less fun.

10 Men have to have the courage to be sexy, to be attractive. Sometimes men hide themselves. I guess they're afraid that they can't be sexy because they're men.

BLAZERS

CHAPTER 3

As men finally begin to embrace elegance again, leaving their wrinkled, untucked selves behind, the sport coat has emerged as the new hoodie. In fact, the blazer is perhaps the single most significant piece of clothing in a man's wardrobe, not to mention one of the most versatile. It is perfectly suited to our ever-fluctuating dress code. The navy blazer is your little black dress. Just don't accessorize with heels.

BLAZER BASICS

(1) THE DETAILS

Blazers are all about details, whether it's ribbon lapels, striped-silk linings under the collar, or embroidery. They can be playful without being embarrassing. (We hope.)

(2) THE FABRIC

Blazers are available in nearly every imaginable material from wool and cotton to corduroy and velvet. Every man should own a summer sport coat, in either linen or light-weight cotton and several others for the cooler seasons.

(3) THE PATTERNS

The simplest, most fail-safe pattern for a blazer is the windowpane plaid, which is essentially just a series of squares that run across the coat. Then there's glen plaid, herringbone, houndstooth, and Prince of Wales check—all classics.

(4) THE POCKETS

If you want a blazer to appear more casual, try patch pockets instead of the usual flap or jetted style. A patch pocket is sewn onto the jacket instead of being cut into the cloth. Because the whole pocket is visible, it is a little less dressy and a lot more appealing, especially on a single-breasted blazer.

(5) SINGLE-BREASTED VS. DOUBLE-BREASTED

As with suits, the choice between a single or double-breasted blazer is strictly one of preference. Both are perfectly acceptable, but double-breasted is more formal and harder to pull off.

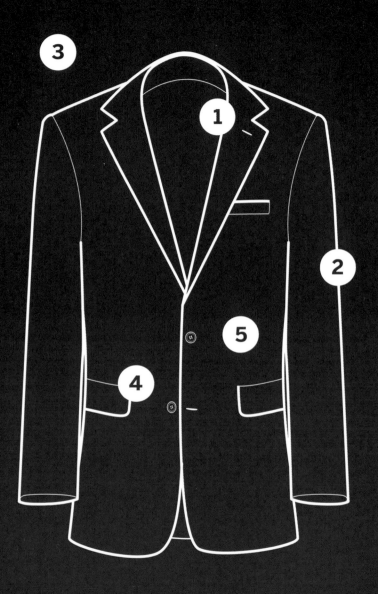

THE PERFECT BLAZER

In theory, the navy blazer is a rather uncomplicated piece of clothing. That said, it can be remarkably different depending on fabric, fit, and style. You want to find as rich a shade of navy blue as possible. Duller tones tend to look cheap. You want your go-to sport coat to be plush and convey warmth. Whether of linen, wool, or cashmere, the right navy blazer will always make you look like you put in more effort than you actually did. Pair it with shirts in bright white, soft blues and pinks, or any shade of gray. Just avoid crests, and unless you're piloting a yacht, pass on the brass.

OPTIONS

SEERSUCKER

Long the uniform of elitist preps and bourbon-soaked Southerners, the seersucker jacket has become a summer classic.

CORDUROY

In a deep chocolate brown, rich maroon, and other warm hues the corduroy blazer is a great winter staple.

PEAK LAPEL

If you want a dressier blazer, choose peak lapels over notched.

PLAID

If you feel up for plaid, we recommend keeping it simple: Wear it with a white shirt and jeans. Bold may be beautiful, but too bold is ugly.

TWEED

Evocative of fox hunts, tweed blazers are elegant in any color or texture. Elbow patches are optional.

VELVET

Velvet makes such a strong statement that anything you accompany it with should be understated. Keep the colors to a minimum.

KHAKI

The khaki blazer is a modern-day classic. Opt for slim, brushed-cotton styles and never, ever pair it with khaki pants.

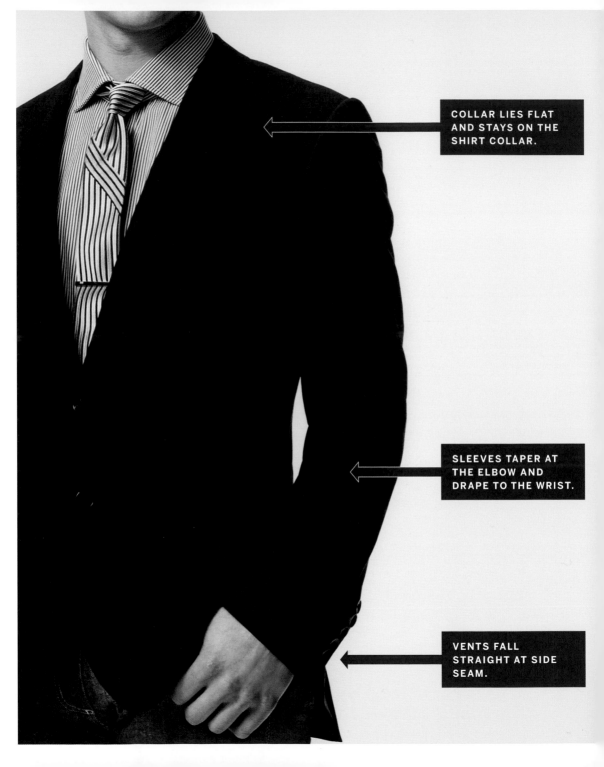

COLLAR LIES FLAT AND STAYS ON THE SHIRT COLLAR.

SLEEVES TAPER AT THE ELBOW AND DRAPE TO THE WRIST.

VENTS FALL STRAIGHT AT SIDE SEAM.

THE PERFECT FIT

SLIM VERSUS RELAXED

Because a blazer is more casual than a suit, you have more freedom with the fit. Loose layering requires a roomier, more relaxed jacket. If you want a crisper, more formal look, opt for slimmer tailoring.

THE SLEEVES

Sleeve length should leave room for about a quarter inch of shirt cuff to show.

THE VENTS

Vents allow for a more forgiving fit. A single center vent works better if you like a slim profile. Double vents will give you more volume around the pants to make room for that sweater. They are good for bigger guys (who should avoid a double-breasted jacket at all costs).

THE BUTTONS

Three-button blazers may help the vertically challenged feel a little taller. A one- or two-button style will bring the oversize guy back into proportion.

! In the 1880s English cricket clubs began making use of brightly colored and patterned sport jackets. **Some of the jackets were so vibrant that onlookers began referring to them as "blazers."**

DRESS UP, DRESS DOWN

How to wear one navy blazer for three different occasions.

Ⓐ TO AN AFTERNOON PARTY
Pair a navy jacket with pressed khakis, a tie, a crisp white pocket square, and you can wear it to any dressy daytime event.

B

TO THE BOARDROOM
The dark-blue blazer becomes less preppy and more business-appropriate when worn over a contrast shirt, with wool trousers, and polished black cap toes.

C

ON A DATE
For a laid-back weeknight out, skip the tie and wear a navy jacket with a collared shirt, dark jeans, and lace-ups.

HOW TO PULL OFF

A Blazer With Jeans

The blazer with jeans is a 21st-century classic. There are plenty of ways to embrace the combination—from subtle to bold.

● ○ ○

BEGINNER
Wear a blazer over a collared white shirt with jeans and loafers or sneakers.

● ● ○

INTERMEDIATE
Wake up a navy blazer with a bold gingham-check shirt. Add a knit tie for texture and contrast the dressiness with jeans in a dark wash.

● ● ●

ADVANCED
Try a lush velvet-corduroy blazer paired with moleskin pants and suede loafers. Texture is the uncharted territory of the well-dressed man.

DON'TS

DON'T DO TOO BUSY

It's a blazer, not a billboard. If you want to demonstrate your risk-taking personality, find another venue.

DON'T HOLD ON
Some pieces of clothing actually look better frayed and faded, but blazers are not on that list. Once a jacket's lost its structure and color, it's time to get yourself a new one.

DON'T WEAR POOR-FITTING BLAZERS
It's not the blazer's fault you don't know what your size is. Clothes that fit are so much more comfortable, let alone stylish. Give them a try.

DON'T FLIP UP YOUR COLLAR INDOORS
Hey, James Dean, put your collar down. There's nothing wrong with using your sport jacket like a jacket. If there's a chill, close the lapels over each other and enjoy the extra warmth. But once you get inside, put your collar down.

DON'T WEAR LEATHER BLAZERS
Unless you're on your way to make a collection for La Famiglia, stay away from leather.

HOW TO BUY

START WITH BASIC BLAZERS—BLUE OR MULTICOLOR CHECK—THAT GIVE YOU A LOT OF OPTIONS. WHEN YOU'VE GOT TWO OR THREE OF THOSE (AND THAT WILL GET YOU THROUGH A SURPRISINGLY LARGE NUMBER OF OCCASIONS) INDULGE YOURSELF IN THE JACKET THAT TURNS HEADS.

A WORD ABOUT FABRICS

Blazers are all about fun, but think carefully about how you're going to wear that khaki blazer before you buy it. Middle-of-the-road fabrics like blue wool have a lot of range. But the outer edges of the spectrum—velvet on one side and khaki on the other—require skill to pull off.

PRICE POINTS STILL MATTER.

So, you're better off spending a lot more on a conservative, versatile blazer (yes, the boring blue one), and less on fashion whims. Over time, you'll find that the old standby not only gives you good value but it will free up cash over the long haul for impulse buys.

WHEN YOU TRY ON YOUR BLAZER BRING A SWEATER WITH YOU AND PUT IT ON FIRST. THERE'S A GOOD CHANCE YOU'RE GOING TO DO SOME LAYERING WITH EITHER A SUMMER- OR WINTER-WEIGHT JACKET. MAKE SURE YOU HAVE THAT EXTRA MARGIN OF SAFETY BY TRYING THE BLAZER ON WITH SOMETHING EXTRA UNDERNEATH.

JEWELRY SHOPS AND VINTAGE STORES HAVE SOME GREAT BUTTONS, SO DO OLD-TIME HABERDASHERIES. WHEN YOU GET A PAIR OF BUTTONS THAT YOU LOVE, IT'S SIMPLE TO REPLACE THE EXISTING ONES ON YOUR JACKET TO GET A CUSTOM LOOK.

MAP OF THE WELL-DRESSED MAN

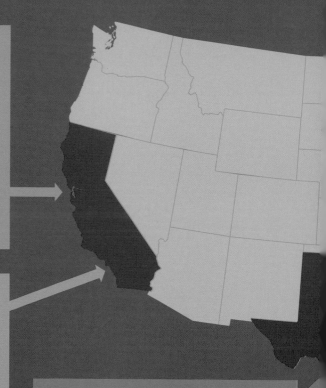

SAN FRANCISCO

Local Style: Relaxed luxury
Cocktail: Negroni
Accessory: White BlackBerry
Getaway: Pescadero
Secret Pleasure: Macchiatos in the back room of Tosca Café
Gentlemanly Act: Keeping the bumper stickers off the Prius
Well-dressed outfit: Gray flannel with brown suede shoes or jeans with a cashmere tweed jacket

LOS ANGELES

Local Style: Totally casual
Cocktail: Vodka gimlet
Accessory: James Perse shirt
Getaway: Alameda Padre Serra, Santa Barbara
Secret Pleasure: Bar-hopping downtown
Gentlemanly Act: Avoiding name-dropping
Well-Dressed outfit: $500 sweatshirt over $300 jeans

DALLAS

Local Style: Big and Brawny
Cocktail: Tequila neat
Accessory: Filson bag
Getaway: Belize
Secret Pleasure: Dove hunting
Gentlemanly Act: Avoiding political discussions
Well-Dressed Outfit: Bright, bold patterns and luxurious fabrics

CHICAGO

Local Style: Conservative but dressy
Cocktail: Gin martini
Accessory: Loro Piana gloves
Weekend Getaway: Door County, Wisconsin
Secret Pleasure: Movies at Music Box Theater
Gentlemanly Act: Taking off Cubs hat indoors
Well-dressed outfit: Pinstripe suits with white shirt and skull-and-bones motif pocket square

NEW YORK

Local Style: Cosmopolitan
Cocktail: Rye Manhattan
Accessory: Barber black wing tips
Getaway: North Fork of Long Island
Gentlemanly Act: Putting the BlackBerry away in a restaurant
Well-dressed outfit: Jay Kos blue blazer with jeans and gingham shirt

MIAMI

Local Style: Keeping cool
Cocktail: Mojito
Accessory: Vintage Ray-Bans
Getaway: Cuba
Guilty Pleasure: Sailing
Gentlemanly Act: Wearing a suit to dinner
Well-dressed outfit: Seersucker suit with French-blue shirt

TIES

CHAPTER 4

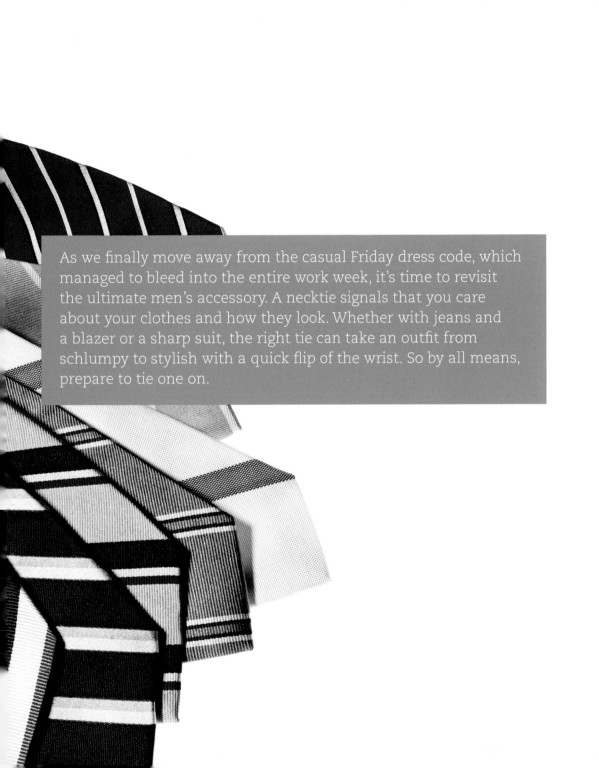

As we finally move away from the casual Friday dress code, which managed to bleed into the entire work week, it's time to revisit the ultimate men's accessory. A necktie signals that you care about your clothes and how they look. Whether with jeans and a blazer or a sharp suit, the right tie can take an outfit from schlumpy to stylish with a quick flip of the wrist. So by all means, prepare to tie one on.

OPTIONS

PRINT

Print ties add visual interest and color to your wardrobe. Just stay away from novelty patterns.

SOLID COLOR

Solid-color ties are underrated. They look particularly sophisticated with striped shirts.

BRIGHT

Balance playful, brightly colored ties with equally eye-catching pocket squares or socks.

KNIT

Knit ties add texture. And contrary to popular opinion, you can wear them year-round.

SMALL PATTERN

Keep your neckwear tasteful, not overpowering, with a tiny houndstooth or microdot pattern.

STRIPE

Striped ties, worn with a navy blazer and a crisp white shirt, are a classic combination.

VARIEGATED STRIPE

Essential accessories don't have to be boring. The variegated stripe adds stylish pizzazz.

POLKA DOT

Dots used to be exceedingly popular. Their extreme versatility will make them so again.

THE KNOT SHOULD REST SNUGLY ON YOUR THROAT BETWEEN THE POINTS OF THE COLLAR.

NO KNOT IS COMPLETE WITHOUT A DIMPLE.

THE TIP OF THE TIE SHOULD HIT THE MIDDLE OF YOUR BELT BUCKLE.

THE PERFECT FIT

THE RIGHT LENGTH

Bigger isn't better when it comes to ties. Rule # 1: The bottom of your tie should never extend below your waistline. Some men choose to tuck a tie into their pants, which is not a sin, but not recommended. If you're vertically challenged, you can let the tail—the thinner back portion of the tie—hang longer and tuck it into your pants.

THE KNOT

The knot you choose depends mostly on the shape of your shirt collar. Spread collars need a larger knot to fill the gap. While there are dozens of variations on the tie knot, if you can believe it, only one really matters. The four-in-hand is the basic, and best, knot, one that can be worn successfully with all collar types. Windsor knots are overrated, and as such, should be avoided. It's a myth that the Duke of Windsor tied a Windsor knot. He simply had his haberdasher use thicker silk.

WELL-MADE

A properly knotted tie is meant to arc from the neck a bit. It's easier to accomplish this with a well-made silk tie, but a tab collar or tie bar will assist in achieving the same effect.

THE WIDTH

Tie widths tend to vary from one year to the next. You can try to keep up with the comings and goings of a fickle fashion flock, but with miles of ties out there—and the fact that a well-cared-for one can last a lifetime—you are better off finding a style that fits your face and frame.

THE DIMPLE

Much overlooked is the dimple, which should lie directly below the knot (see page 82). A tie without a dimple is like pants without a fly. It absolutely needs to be there.

! Cambridge University physicists Thomas Fink and Yong Mao determined that **there are 85 different ways to tie the conventional necktie.**

KNOTS 101

Four-in-hand

1. Place the tie around your collar with the wider side draped on your right and under your right hand. Take each side in each hand midway down the tie. The skinny side should be about a foot shorter than the wide side.

2. Put your right hand over your left, pull under and across—you've just established the length of the tie.

3. Now flip the tie from your right shoulder across to your left and hold the knot in your left hand.

4. A great knot comes down to tension—and a dimple. Carefully reach through the knot with your right hand and pull up, then feed the tie down and into itself. You will see the knot forming nicely.

5. To finish the tie properly, pull gently from just beneath the knot to achieve the right tension. Pinching the center of the tie between thumb and forefinger is the best way to go here. That way you'll create that all-important dimple.

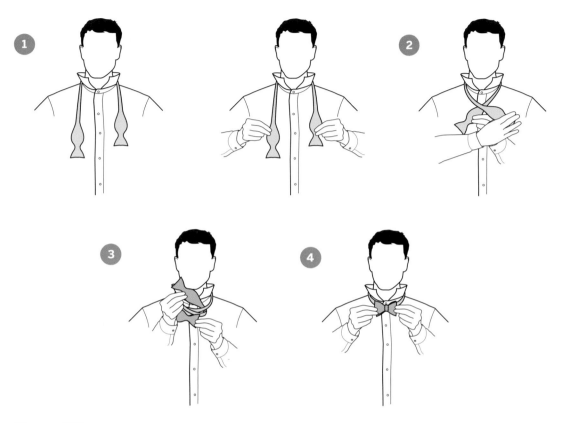

Bow Tie

Believe it or not, knotting a bow tie isn't that difficult to master. It may take a few attempts, but once you get it down, it's no sweat.

1. Start with a simple right over left.

2. Take the left side and fold it at the throat into half a bow.

3. Take the right up and over so it hangs down the middle of the bow. Fold the right end horizontally and slip it through the knot behind the left.

4. Pull the loops at each end to tighten the bow. What follows is a lot of wiggling to even out the ends and make your bow smooth and balanced. A bow tie shouldn't be perfect, or you won't get credit for having tied it.

Remember, bow ties look best when worn with a tux. There's a pretty significant putz factor otherwise. So unless you're changing your name to Redenbacher, do yourself a favor, and stay away.

EVOLUTION OF THE TIE

China's first emperor is placed in a tomb guarded by terra-cotta warriors, all adorned with silk neckwear.

Carriage drivers who guide four horses wear their scarves tied in a distinctive knot. The four-in-hand knot emerges in England.

Jesse Langsdorf revolutionizes the tie by cutting a piece of cloth at 45 degrees, thus having the tie drape better and last longer. This method is still used by tie manufacturers.

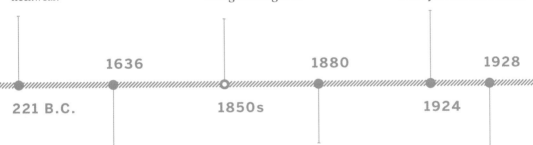

1636　　**1880**　　**1928**

221 B.C.　　**1850s**　　**1924**

Croatian soldiers wearing bright silk scarves are presented to King Louis XIII of France. By the time of Louis XIV's reign, the neckwear becomes the accessory of choice in the French court and the word *cravat* is born.

Oxford University's rowing club invents the first school tie by using the ribbon in their hats to form a tie.

Clip-on tie invented.

The power shirt replaces the power tie, as shirts become louder and brighter.

The Rat Pack popularizes the one-inch tie in *Ocean's 11*.

In a sea of dark, narrow ties, Ralph Lauren starts a neckwear revolution by introducing the 4-inch wide tie. Ties would get super-wide into the seventies.

Ronald Reagan is elected. The new Republican majority comes to Washington, bringing first the red power tie, then the yellow.

Jeremy Piven shows up at the Emmys wearing an ascot. He looks like an idiot.

1946		1971		1997	2000	
	1960	1967	1980	1999		2006

Extra-gaudy ties in loud patterns are the trend. It is attributed to a reaction to an unsettled postwar world.

The bolo is made the official neck-wear of Arizona.

Corporate restructurings and rise of the dotcoms bring casual dress to work. Throwing out one's tie is a sign of "getting it."

Who Wants to be a Millionaire host Regis Philbin sports a monochromatic tie-shirt combo, sending neckwear sales soaring.

HOW TO PULL OFF

Prints With Prints

Dressing well has everything to do with finding new ways to combine the components of your wardrobe. Each new piece you buy sets up dozens of possibilities. Nowhere is this more important than with shirts and ties. But you're going to have to learn some basic rules.

BEGINNER

Match your colors. Make sure your shirt and tie share a common color. A word of caution: Beware the monochromatic look. While you want there to be some of the same color in both, the exact color is not recommended. When starting out, just be sure there are similar tones in both the tie and the shirt.

INTERMEDIATE

Balance patterns: The easy rule of thumb is to use striped ties to offset patterned shirts and printed ties (make sure the print is a different scale) to offset stripes. Dots go with everything.

ADVANCED

Pattern mixing is allowed. When you feel up to it, try a striped tie with a striped shirt. Just make sure the stripes are different sizes. Avoid this look when wearing a pinstripe suit. A common color theme is wise here but not necessary. The same rules apply for patterns and checks. Busy isn't bad, but you don't want to get crazy here. Too much activity may cause seizures.

DON'TS

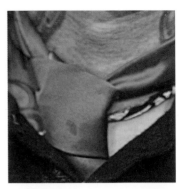

DON'T WEAR A GIANT KNOT

You don't want a knot that's going to compete with your head. A giant knot on a too-thick tie will immediately overpower your suit.

DON'T GET TOO LOOSE OR TOO MESSY

It's perfectly acceptable to unbutton your shirt collar and loosen your tie a bit, but there's a limit to how loose it should be. An inch-and-a half below the Adam's apple is appropriate. If the knot settles somewhere between your pecs, then you might as well take the tie off. You don't want to wander around looking like you've just been lassoed.

HOW TO BUY

A TIE IS ONLY AS GOOD AS THE FABRIC IT'S MADE OF. A GOOD TIE IS MADE FROM THICK, STRONG SILK AND LINED WITH MINIMAL MATERIAL TO GIVE IT A GOOD "HAND."

Remember, ties are meant to accent your outfit, not overpower it. It's about nuance, not neon.

The best ties are called seven-fold ties. They are literally one piece of silk folded seven times and sewn into a tie. Do you need one? Not really. But it's nice to know that they're out there.

Ties allow us to show some personal style in a sea of navy suits. Like shoes, they can dress up an outfit or make it more relaxed. Most men don't have nearly enough ties in their wardrobe. Start with a solid navy tie. Buy some ties with stripes in two colors. Then branch out into some basic patterns. Remember to get a conservative dominant color: blue, brown, red, or even yellow. The knit tie has seen a resurgence in popularity and works well in many situations.

RULES
OF STYLE

Michael
Kors

1 **What works for men is mixing something rugged with something indulgent.** If you're wearing a floor-length sheepskin coat and a 10-ply sweater, wear it with torn-up jeans. Mix something high with something low.

2 **Guys are more secure about mixing now.** It used to be either "work" or "weekend" wear or "bad date." A bad-date outfit is too much Bordeaux—a wine-colored leather jacket with a short-sleeve slinky knit. For a lot of men, the idea of what you wear on a date is something that feels sexual. The reality is, you look like you're wearing your girlfriend's blouse in a big size.

3 **The rules for dressing have changed.** Everyone is 35 today. Brad Pitt is 40. Kurt Russell is 53. Jude Law is 31. And I think they're all 35. The younger guy is wearing tailored pieces to look sophisticated. And the older guy is going for a more casual piece to feel younger. It all kind of comes together, and the world is 35. Except me. I'm 85.

4 **I take issue with mandals.** It looks like someone basically took the top of a shoebox and put two straps on. It's Fred Flintstone. They're hideous.

5 **For most men, shorts work unless you have total pelican legs.** You can go to the gym 100 times a week, but either you have good legs or you don't. If you do have good legs, they stay good. If so, I say go for it. Myself, I'm a Judy Garland kind of guy. Everything else has gone to seed, but the legs are still good.

6 **A tan makes you feel skinnier, just like wearing dark clothes does.** There's something about a man with a tan—it says a guy's either the boss or a bum. He's not middle management.

7 **I believe in clipping and pruning, but not in shaving.** I've even seen men who shave the hair on their forearms, which is a strange look. Like they were eating fondue and got too close to the flame.

8 **If you're not great-looking, wear a fabulous watch, carry expensive luggage, wear sunglasses.** It worked for Onassis. Even if you don't have a big bank account, you look like you do.

9 **All men should own a black cashmere turtleneck, a high-quality tropical-weight black suit, black driving loafers, and the most expensive white shirt you can afford.**

10 **I won't wear a bow tie with a tuxedo because I feel like someone is going to order a drink from me.** For most men, the neck is not an easy area. I think you have to be really skinny or really fat—someone like Jude Law or Philip Seymour Hoffman.

11 **Matching head-to-toe sports outfits freak me out.** It works for Dave Beckham because he is actually coming off the field. He is not an accountant or a stockbroker running around doing errands.

SUITS

CHAPTER 5

It's no coincidence that *suit* is a four-letter word. Think about it for a second. If someone refers to you as a "suit," he's certainly not paying you a compliment. Popular culture dictates that the guy in a suit is the dork, the killjoy. The guy in the suit represents the Establishment. But since when is that such a bad thing? Web 2.0 has spawned countless invaluable lifestyle contributions, but it's also created a generation of slobs. The days of chinos and pull-overs at the office are over. It's time to start dressing like a gentle-man again, and a great suit is the first step toward reclaiming your place at the top of the sartorial food chain. The suit is the most important set of clothing in a man's wardrobe, and it should be worn proudly—and regularly. The right suit has the ability to tran-scend mere dressing. Like Superman's cape, a suit brings other-wise hidden attributes to the surface: power, confidence, authority. No wonder it's been the staple of masculine dress for the better part of a century. So the next time some punk in frayed cords and a faux vintage tee gives you a sideways glance, feel free to unleash as many four-letter words as you can think of.

SUIT BASICS

① THE SHOULDERS

A good suit starts at the shoulders. It should fit your posture and flatter your frame. If your suit jacket doesn't make you look better when you put it on, you're wearing the wrong one.

② THE LAPEL

Avoid narrow and extra wide and keep it somewhere in the middle. Also consider whether you prefer a notched lapel—which is customary—or a more dramatic peaked version.

③ THE BUTTONS

Suit snobs pay close attention to the buttons on the sleeve of a suit jacket. Most suits, even those from top European designers, have sleeve buttons that don't actually unbutton but are strictly for show. The best suits have working button holes on the sleeves. And while you're not likely to ever see anyone rolling up the sleeve of the suit jacket unless his name is Michael Jackson, some flashier types like undoing these buttons in order to show off the superior hand tailoring of their garment.

④ THE PATTERN

Stripes and checks are the most popular patterns for suits—though these are often so subtle they are not noticeable from even a short distance. A better suit carefully matches where the patterns meet and overlap, with stripes continuing across the seams perfectly.

⑤ THE POCKETS

Most suits are delivered with the pockets sewn shut. Pull them open, but don't load them with your PDA, keys, or iPod as this will ruin the silhouette.

⑥ THE LINING

Subtle or shocking, a good lining, like functional button holes on the sleeve, allows suit junkies another opportunity to demonstrate their sartorial flair.

⑦ THE STITCHING

Superior suits are hand-stitched by a tailor. Although fusing—a fancy word for the suit being glued together—is commonplace for off-the-rack suits, a truly handmade suit will be sewn by artisans. This will be reflected in the price.

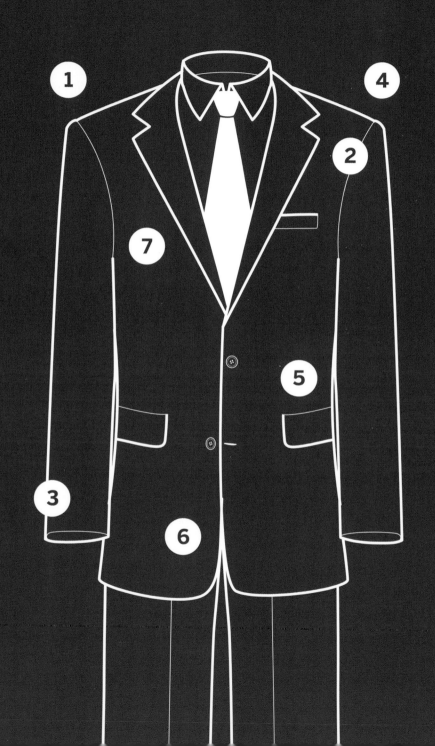

THE PERFECT SUIT

A cheap suit is as easy to spot in a crowd as a bad toupee. As a rule, it's far better to have two great suits than five mediocre ones. Start with a rich midnight blue, a few shades darker than the average navy. This suit will transition beautifully from day to night, and can be worn with both black and dark-brown shoes. It goes with just about everything. In fact, you'd have to try extremely hard to find a shirt-and-tie combo that clashes with the right dark-blue suit. Choose a solid blue or try a subtle pattern, be it herringbone, windowpane, or the classic pinstripe. No other suit will give you as much mileage. Every suit wardrobe should begin here.

OPTIONS

BLACK

Not just for undertakers anymore. Worn with a soft blue shirt, the black suit can feel decidedly informal. Try a crisp white shirt and skinny black tie, and you'll understand why this look is such a classic.

GRAY

Next to midnight blue, a gray suit is the essential component of any well-curated closet. Nothing is so versatile: Whether worn with black, brown, or cordovan shoes, you can wear the same gray suit every day of the week. As long as you vary shoes and shirt and tie, no one will be the wiser.

HERRINGBONE

A classic gentleman's suit, herringbone gets its name from the zigzag pattern of the twill used to make it. Generally, this is a heavier suit, which is at its best in the winter.

COTTON

Warm weather isn't an excuse to dress down. Cotton, brushed or otherwise, will let you maintain your style without suffocating.

LINEN

Most suits are wool, and no matter how lightweight they may be, are too warm to be worn during the summer. The linen suit offers an antidote to overheating when the mercury starts to rise, and can be worn with more casual shoes, even sneakers, if it's appropriate for the occasion.

PRINCE OF WALES

A glen-check suit with a light-blue overplaid, is the classic Prince of Wales. A French-blue shirt will bring out the best in it.

WINDOWPANE

An elegant alternative to pinstripes, a subtle window-pane plaid is a beautiful addition to any wardrobe.

SEAMS FALL ALONG YOUR SHOULDER.

THE SUIT SHOULD HAVE A TRIM LINE THAT FOLLOWS THE LINES OF YOUR BODY.

YOUR SLEEVE LENGTH SHOULD ALLOW SOME SHIRT CUFF TO SHOW.

THE PERFECT FIT

You could have the most expensive suit on the market, but if it doesn't fit properly, you're going to look like a farmer. A suit should be neither too tight nor too loose, it should gently hug the body, but not restrict you in any way.

A suit jacket should pull smoothly across your back when buttoned. The lapels are meant to lay flat across the chest. Some padding in the shoulders, we're not talking David Byrne here, can help fill out your frame. Needless to say, there is no one style that works best for all men. Take your time. Do your research. And whatever you do, trust the mirror. No matter how much your wife or girlfriend (if you're still shopping with your mother at this point, finding the right suit is the least of your problems) tell you how amazing you look, if you aren't feeling it, try something else.

THE ENGLISH FIT

The British have a rich tradition of impeccable tailoring. While Savile Row has changed significantly over the years, there's still no place like it. English suits tend to fit close to the body, accentuating a defined waist, strong chest, and naturally sloping shoulders. These features are exaggerated by the British taste for double vents that flare at the bottom of the coat. High armholes, trim sleeves, and tapered pants only add to the lean look. English suits tend to hug the body without feeling, or looking, tight.

THE ITALIAN FIT

Europeans developed a very different suit with a high, padded shoulder and longer jacket. The Italian suit drapes more than the British and is accented by narrower pants, which are often worn much higher on the ankle.

THE ALL-AMERICAN FIT

Classic American style emerged in the 1950s with the Ivy League look. It reached its epitome in the Sack suit, a three-button model that is more forgiving than the tailored looks from across the Atlantic. This Brooks Brothers look has lower armholes, three buttons, and a natural, sloping shoulder and is generally more relaxed and informal.

! **Abraham Lincoln** was wearing a black bespoke suit from Brooks Brothers when he was assassinated. **The company didn't make black suits for the next 133 years.**

Fit Tips

THE LAPELS

The lapels of your suit jacket are meant to lay flat across your chest. If they bow out even a little, then the suit is too tight. Make sure the notch on your lapel is close to your tie knot, otherwise you'll look lopsided.

THE BUTTONS

The number of buttons on a suit has more to do with preference than fit. On a three-button suit, the only button that gets used is the waist, or middle, button. You may be tempted to button the top button in a rakish way, but resist this urge. When there are two buttons, fasten only the top one. An elegant alternative is the single-button suit, which offers a sharp, formal look.

  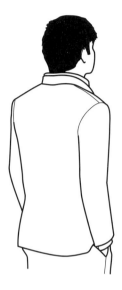

THE VENTS

Double vents make it easier to pull the jacket close to your frame, particularly if you're solidly built. Single vents keep the silhouette slim, but allow for easy access to your pockets.

DOUBLE-BREASTED VS. SINGLE-BREASTED

The single-breasted suit should be your default choice for both work and play. The double-breasted version is a dashing, continental choice that's chic, but not for men on the shorter or heavier side as it adds fabric to your midsection. One other tip: Always keep it buttoned.

DRESS UP, DRESS DOWN

How to wear one gray suit for four different occasions.

(A) AT THE OFFICE

Some men think an open collar means they look more relaxed, but in reality they appear like they've missed a step. If you are wearing a suit and a white or blue shirt to the office, then you should always choose a tie.

(B) LATE NIGHT OUT

When worn with a strong patterned or darker-color shirt, the suit makes the transition to night.

C MEETING THE PARENTS
Lose the tie and wear a sweater under your jacket.

D SUNDAY BRUNCH
Pair with a casual polo shirt and sneakers for the weekend.

EVOLUTION OF THE SUIT

The term *leisure suit* is added to Merriam-Webster's dictionary

The Prince of Wales tours the world and becomes an instant celebrity. Men everywhere want to imitate his suit's look: a full chest and a pinched waist.

Robert Mitchum in films like *His Kind of Woman* demonstrates the new vogue for big shoulders and straight waists.

The Beatles take *The Ed Sullivan Show* stage in slim mod suits.

Talking Heads front man David Byrne wears the Big Suit in the music documentary *Stop Making Sense*.

1942

1956

1977

1920

1951

1964 **1975**

1983

The zoot suit gains popularity despite the War Production Board's wool rationing guidelines. Tailors and manufacturers flout regulations to supply the demand for the baggy outfit.

The work uniform of the 1950s is encapsulated by the release of *The Man in the Gray Flannel Suit*.

John Travolta immortalizes the high-waisted, three-piece white disco suit in *Saturday Night Fever*.

Two fictional Miami cops, Sonny Crockett and Rico Tubbs, in unconstructed pastel suits with pushed-up sleeves capture the nation's imagination.

Reservoir Dogs is released, sparking record sales of black suits with skinny ties.

Men in Black is released, sparking record sales of black suits with skinny ties.

Rappers like Jay-Z and Diddy go from street to chic, as they embrace bespoke tailoring.

Savile Row tailors report that the majority of their business comes from American men.

1987

1994

2001

2006

1984

1992

1997

2005

2007

Michael Douglas, as Gordon Gekko, glamorizes the power suit in *Wall Street*.

Dot-com boom makes the suit an endangered species.

Justin Timberlake wears a stone-washed denim suit to the MTV Video Music Awards, elevating bad taste to a high art.

Justin Timberlake endeavors to establish himself as an arbiter of good taste by launching his own fashion label, William Rast. Denim suits are not offered.

HOW TO PULL OFF

The Khaki Suit

While this perfect summer suit doesn't have to be kept in the closet after dark, you need to accessorize correctly to make a khaki suit as versatile as a dark one.

● ○ ○

● ● ○

● ● ●

BEGINNER
Khaki suits are made for daytime events with relaxed dress codes. Reinforce the informal aesthetic with a chambray shirt, a thin sweater vest, and tan leather shoes or spotless white sneakers.

INTERMEDIATE
Sand-colored cotton's preppy roots make it a perfect backdrop for bright color. Pair a khaki suit with a green-and-white striped tie, a collared shirt, or a polo in a sherbet hue like tangerine or raspberry. Avoid overkill by steering clear of whale pants and sailboat motifs.

ADVANCED
A khaki suit can look just as elegant as a tux. The trick is to skip the bright colors and stick with an otherwise black-and-white palette: a crisp white shirt, a black tie adorned with a silver tie bar, and a white pocket square.

DON'TS

DON'T WEAR SUITS WITH TOO MANY BUTTONS

Anything more than three buttons on a single-breasted suit has disaster written all over it. Think MC Hammer. He used to own this look. And now? Well, he doesn't own much of anything anymore.

DON'T SETTLE FOR BAD FIT

A suit just isn't a suit until it fits you. There's nothing worse than looking like you're wearing bad hand-me-downs.

DON'T GO SHINY

Where did all the silk and sharkskin go? Don't know, but we're not complaining. If you want to wear a shiny suit, join a band. Offstage they should be avoided.

DON'T BUY CHEAP SUITS

It may look like a bargain, but you'll pay for it in the end. When building a suit wardrobe, remember that quality trumps quantity. One great suit is better than two cheap ones. The right navy or gray suit can be worn with a mix of shirts, sweaters, and shoes to make it seem like you're wearing a different outfit every day.

HOW TO BUY

OFF-THE-RACK   Know at least two configurations of suit shape, lapels, and buttons that are flattering to your form. Having a good sense of what works for you will make it a lot easier to concentrate on the important things. Sometimes it's as simple as knowing a designer or tailor whose aesthetic reflects your needs. Just because you're buying a suit off the rack, doesn't mean it won't require a fair bit of tailoring. Make sure you know your size in both American and European measurements—the numbers will be different. When shopping for suits, it's important to wear a collared shirt, a belt, and the appropriate shoes. That way the tailor can fit the arm length to your own shirt cuff and the pant break to your shoes.

CUSTOM   A full-on custom suit is a collaboration between client and tailor. Each tailor has his own style so you are better off finding a tailor whose work you admire than trying to make a tailor bend toward your imagination. Once you've found a sympathetic sartorial soulmate, discuss what you want to use the suit for and what details he can add to make it special. Custom tailors are artisans, if you find the right tailor, stick with him.

Made-to-measure allows you to choose the suit fabric, type of lapel, the number of buttons, even the shape of the pocket. Consider it custom with training wheels.

HOW TO ALTER YOUR SUIT   There are some places a tailor can completely remake the suit and others where he can only make a bad situation worse. A suit has to fit correctly on the shoulders. Once you've got that happening, the rest is workable. Is the jacket too long for you? The tailor can take it up an inch. Sleeves can be narrowed slightly, especially at the forearm and the waist can be taken in. The pants can get roomier in the seat and opened up in the crotch. The legs can be tapered and length adjusted. Be aware that things like pockets and pleats cannot be reworked. But if you don't like those, you shouldn't be buying the suit in the first place.

POCKET SQUARES CAN ADD A DRESSY ACCENT TO YOUR SUIT. WE RECOMMMEND A SIMPLY FOLDED ONE, QUARTER THE SWATCH OF FABRIC AND SHOW JUST A SLIVER FROM YOUR CHEST POCKET.

KNOW THE CODE

Life is complicated. There is a greater variety of events in more diverse settings than ever before. It may seem like anything goes—but there are still some worthwhile rules to follow. Here's a stab at some.

CHURCH AND STATE   Serious occasions demand appropriate attire. Dark clothes with high-contrast accessories: generally a dark suit and white shirt with a dark tie and black shoes. The most serious places on earth are courts, houses of worship, and seats of executive power. In these places you never want to be wearing anything that says you're casual.

TRAVEL   People used to dress up when they traveled. They wanted everyone they came into contact with to know that they were respectable, would pay their bills (or tip), and behave properly. It's a fact: Wear suit or tie in most places and you'll get treated with more respect. Any more respect you can get in an airport is worth the effort.

YOUR HOUSE   The closer to home you get, the more casual your clothes become. Black shoes give way to brown, dark suits to light, smooth fabrics to rougher. Inside your own house you should be able to wear anything you like (or nothing at all). But when you invite others into your home, you're making it a public place. Politeness—the concern for the comfort of others—dictates that you create an atmosphere of comfort for your guests. That usually means getting dressed up to their level rather than having them come dressed as if they were in their own homes.

SUMMER WEDDING   Your friends are getting married on the beach. They want to feel the sand between their toes as they say their vows. Good for them. They'll be in a tuxedo and a wedding dress. What are you going to wear? We suggest a light-color, lightweight suit with a formal tie or white linen shirt.

There was a time when *formal* and *semi-formal* had real meaning to any man who heard the term. *Formal* meant tails, a white vest, and white tie. If you had them, you were expected to wear medals and decorations too. *Semi-formal* meant you could wear a tuxedo, what the British still call a dinner jacket. In other words, a ball was formal; a dinner was semi-formal. Well, that's not our world. You're more likely to read *Black Tie* or *Black Tie Optional* on an invitation. What does that mean?

Black Tie

Get out your tux. If it's black tie, it means your host wants it to be a special occasion. Make him feel special that you showed up. And unless you know the crowd you're going to see there, you might want to stick with basic black and white. Reserve the red-velvet jacket for your friends.

Black Tie Optional

This is still a dressy event. Your host expects some folks to show up in a tuxedo. He'll probably wear one himself. But he's giving you permission to wear something appropriate to the occasion but not as cumbersome. A very-dark suit, white shirt, and solid dark tie are appropriate. A white pocket square folded neatly and peeking out of the pocket is a nice grace note. Black patent-leather shoes will get you extra credit.

No Instructions

It's okay to call. In fact, you might be doing your host a favor. In all the to and fro that goes into putting on a party, he may have failed to think about what you would wear. A polite, "What's the dress code for Saturday night?" gives your host the opportunity to describe his ambitions for the party. You can decide what clothes will fit the occasion. If you do call, have the courtesy to follow your host's guidelines. In fact, a good rule for dressing is stick to the high side.

FORMALWEAR

CHAPTER 6

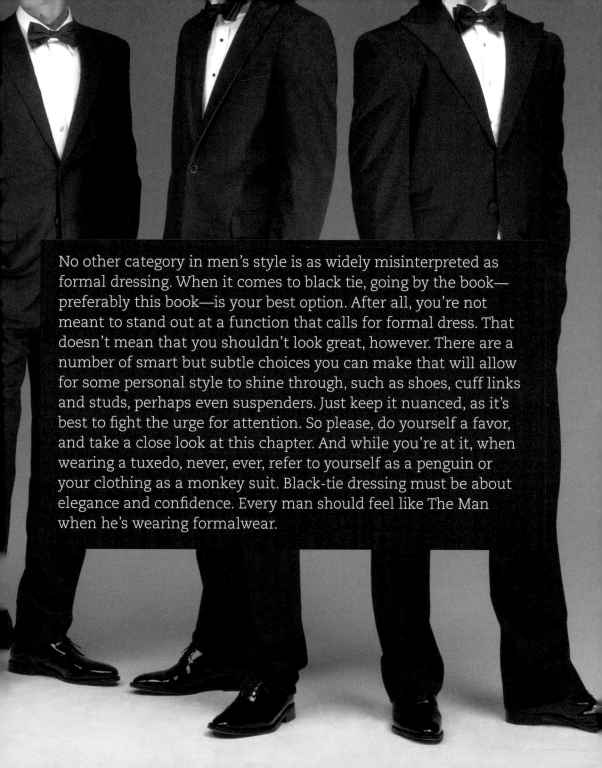

No other category in men's style is as widely misinterpreted as formal dressing. When it comes to black tie, going by the book— preferably this book—is your best option. After all, you're not meant to stand out at a function that calls for formal dress. That doesn't mean that you shouldn't look great, however. There are a number of smart but subtle choices you can make that will allow for some personal style to shine through, such as shoes, cuff links and studs, perhaps even suspenders. Just keep it nuanced, as it's best to fight the urge for attention. So please, do yourself a favor, and take a close look at this chapter. And while you're at it, when wearing a tuxedo, never, ever, refer to yourself as a penguin or your clothing as a monkey suit. Black-tie dressing must be about elegance and confidence. Every man should feel like The Man when he's wearing formalwear.

TUXEDO BASICS

1 THE STRIPE

The tuxedo is descended from a military dress uniform, which explains the stripe down the seam of the pants.

2 SINGLE-BREASTED VS. DOUBLE-BREASTED

Like suits, tuxedos are offered in single and double-breasted silhouettes. And, as with suits, make sure you're a double-breasted build before making yourself a double-breasted guy. Single-breasted tuxedos have traditionally had a rounded, or shawl, collar. While this style has endured and continues to be perfectly acceptable, you can't go wrong with a peaked or even notch lapel these days.

3 THE SHIRT

Wear a well-pressed white dress shirt (preferably French cuff). Warning: Wearing a ruffled shirt is a bold move. You don't want to look like one of the Sweat Hogs on prom night. (If the *Welcome Back, Kotter* reference is lost on you, dig up an old photo of your father at his senior formal, and you'll get the idea.)

4 THE VEST OR CUMMERBUND

You can wear either a vest or a cummerbund under a single-breasted tuxedo but nothing but a shirt under a double-breasted one. Just so you know, the pleats on the cummerbund face up because they're designed to catch any crumbs that may fall. If there's one black-tie component that is truly optional these days, it is the cummerbund. If you do choose to wear a cummerbund or vest, stay away from jazzy patterns like paisley print. Suppress your inner Manilow.

5 THE SHOES

Tuxedos are meant to be worn with tuxedo shoes. You have some flexibility here. Purists will insist on slip-ons, made from silk, velvet, or patent leather. Lace-ups will do just fine, just be sure to give them a high shine.

6 THE TIE

Bow ties used to be a must, but worn properly, the elegant four-in-hand—especially in silver, white, or black—is a suitable alternative. If you're wearing a bow tie, learn to tie a real one. It's not that hard (see p. 83).

TUXEDO SHIRTS? GO TO PAGE 122

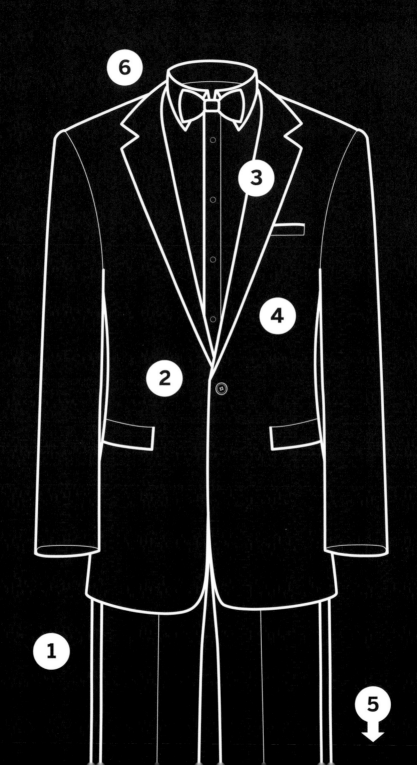

DOUBLE-BREASTED

Too many men who shouldn't be wearing double-breasted suits make the mistake of thinking they can pull off a double-breasted tuxedo.

SHAWL COLLAR

It's the simplicity of the black-and-white outfit that makes it so classy. The rounded shawl collar has long been the classic. You don't need to improve upon it.

SINGLE-BREASTED

A single-breasted tuxedo in a notched or a peaked lapel is as acceptable as the traditional shawl collar.

WHITE DINNER JACKET

If it's summer or you're attending a function in a year-round warm climate, the white dinner jacket is a classy option. Avoid the red carnation—and the red wine.

OPTIONS: SHIRTS AND SHOES

BIB SHIRT

So-called because of the woven oval that extends across the chest, the bib shirt is a solid choice for formal attire.

VELVET

If you're willing to go for it, then go big and be sure to get a pair embroidered with your initials.

BLACK LACE-UPS

A widely acceptable alternative to flashier formal footwear.

PATENT LEATHER

Old-school fashion law dictates that pumps are the proper shoes to wear with a tuxedo. Break this law. If you feel inclined to honor tradition, try a pair of patent-leather slip-ons.

WING COLLAR

A throwback to the 19th century, the wing collar is best suited for white tie and tails. Stick with a turn-down collar.

PLEATED SHIRT

Pleats are the classiest of tuxedo shirts.

TURN-DOWN COLLAR

Simple and elegant, this is the preferred shirt for wearing with a dinner jacket.

BOW TIE

Never use a clip-on. Once you learn to tie a bow (see page 83), you'll never go back.

STRAIGHT TIE

The impossible-to-ignore option. Wearing a four-in-hand tie with a tuxedo is modern and chic.

JACKET FALLS EXACTLY ON THE SHOULDER.

A LITTLE BIT OF CUFF AND YOUR CUFF LINKS SHOULD BE VISIBLE AT THE WRIST.

THE PERFECT FIT

A TUXEDO FITS LIKE A SUIT

As with your suits, fit is everything when it comes to black-tie dressing. Stick with a single-button, single-breasted cut that sits close to your frame. For warm-weather events, try a white dinner jacket if you're feeling particularly confident. (Be sure to pair it with black tuxedo pants. A white suit at a black-tie party is definitely not a good look.)

THE BREAK

It's okay for your pants to have a shorter break than your standard trousers have.

THE FABRIC

In the autumn and winter months, stick with the classic wool fabrics used for your suits. As you'll probably only have one tuxedo in the closet, make sure the wool isn't too heavy. This is a big-ticket item, and you'll want to get the most wear out of the tuxedo.

THE STUDS AND CUFF LINKS

Tuxedo shirts have traditionally required a stud and cuff-link set. These days studs are no longer a must, as going without has become quite common and can present a clean, sophisticated look. The French-cuff shirt, however, should be a staple. Find classic sterling-silver cuff links or perhaps some vintage enamel, as long as the colors are relatively neutral.

JACKET REQUIRED

Unless you're planning to drape your jacket over the shoulders of a shivering female, keep it on.

A WORD ABOUT WEDDING ATTIRE

A morning suit with a cutaway coat is the most formal daytime outfit a man can wear. If you're getting married while the sun is out, the morning suit can be an elegant choice. Wear it with a vest, a striped tie, and oxfords. Leave the top hat and the ascot at home.

CUFF LINKS? GO TO PAGE 240

HOW TO PULL OFF

The Tuxedo

Lose the cummerbund. Unless Henry VIII gnawing on a Flintstones-size chicken leg represents your gold standard for table manners, the cummerbund is superfluous.

If you only wear a tuxedo once or twice a year, make the effort and tie your own bow tie. If you have many social engagements that call for black tie, mix it up a bit and work a straight tie in occasionally. And no matter which tie you choose, go with the turn-down collar.

Never wear a belt with formalwear. Suspenders may seem cool, but most men wear them incorrectly. In order to pull them off successfully, your clothes need to be cut properly. Odds are yours aren't. In reality, your tuxedo pants should have a strong waistband and sidetabs to take the place of suspenders.

BEGINNER
Do you wear a tux once a year? Then stick to the formula. You'll enjoy it, even the ritual cursing as you screw up your bow tie the first time.

INTERMEDIATE
Get the right shoes on and use them to make a statement. If you've got a great family heirloom like a set of studs or gold cuff links, throw those on too.

ADVANCED
If you wear a tuxedo often—more than four times a year—you might want to think about getting some accessories that will break up the monotony: another pair of shoes, a different bow tie, and more than one shirt.

DON'TS

DON'T WEAR COLORED TUXEDOS
This is one case when fashion should be black and white, without any gray area.

DON'T GO TOO SMALL
Make sure your tuxedo fits. Even if it's rented, it is yours for the evening, so take the time to have a tailor give you a once-over.

DON'T TRY TO BRING BACK LOST STYLES
You might think you're sending up the self-serious but you're really just being rude. If an occasion is black tie, you should show up in a tuxedo or send your regrets.

DON'T OVERDO IT
The tuxedo is a fairly rigid form. If you're going to wear one, try to stick to the basic formula.

HOW TO BUY

THINK ABOUT HOW YOU'RE REALLY GOING TO USE YOUR TUXEDO. IF YOU ONLY GO TO A FEW FORMAL EVENTS A YEAR, JUST WEARING A TUX IS SPECIAL ENOUGH. IF YOU'RE GOING OUT A LOT, YOU'LL WANT SOME VARIETY, THINK ABOUT GETTING ANOTHER JACKET— WHITE PERHAPS—OR SOMETHING ELSE TO WORK INTO THE ROTATION.

Remember, your tuxedo should fit like a suit. If you haven't bought one yet, even if you only wear one once a year, it's time to pull the trigger. Owning a tuxedo is the mark of a true gentleman. You shouldn't be renting clothing at this point in your life.

A LITTLE GOES A LONG WAY. USE VERY SUBTLE DETAILS—
HEIRLOOM STUDS, VELVET SHOES, A POCKET SQUARE—TO
GIVE YOU SOME DISTINCTION.

RULES
OF STYLE

Sean
Combs

1 Smooth is a thing you can learn from Sinatra. He looked everybody in the eye. The way he moved—Sinatra was always making statements, but he was never being loud. He didn't have to yell.

2 **You've got to get your smell right.** Walk into an elevator with a beautiful woman in it. If you've got your scent going in the right direction, she's gonna be thinking about you when you leave. That's the way to seal a woman.

3 I don't have a lot of body hair. If I did, I'd get rid of it. For a woman, a wax is absolutely necessary. It makes everything smoother and more attainable. It makes room for all the advances I make when I'm going to please a woman.

4 **Some guys look better in jeans than a suit.** You've got to let your handsome work for you. You've got to accentuate.

5 **Accomplishment is attractive.** There are men who wouldn't make the cover of some "Sexiest Man Alive" issue of a magazine, but they get real appealing when they open their mouths. I'd rather be blessed with that than with looks.

6 **It's better to look like you're wearing something that fits than like you're wearing a trend.**

7 **Women are going to tell you they love a man who's huggable—that they like something they can hold on to—but at the end of the day, nothing compares to a toned body.** There's nothing wrong with letting it all hang out, but when you care, it shows.

8 I'm not just saying this because I'm a black man—I love all my brothers and sisters of other colors—but we are the most flavorful race.

9 I have a "man bag." I'm not gonna lie. Just make sure that if you carry one, it's very, very big, so it doesn't get mistaken for a pocketbook.

10 Don't mess with the cut of your suit too much. Some things are going to look good on you, and some aren't. Leave that up to your tailor.

JEANS

CHAPTER 7

We all have pieces of clothing we're fond of—a perfectly cut suit, an extra-soft cashmere sweater, or a worn-in T-shirt. But nothing comes close to trumping our favorite jeans. The right pair plays a starring role in a man's life. (Take the album cover of Bruce Springsteen's *Born in the U.S.A.*) They've outlasted girlfriends—even wives. It would seem then, that once you find the ideal pair, you're set for life. Not true. By all means, hang on to your beloved 501s, but don't overlook the abundance of new options. After all, now that jeans have become more acceptable cocktail-hour attire, you should probably own more than one pair (depending on the pair).

THE PERFECT PAIR OF JEANS—LEVI'S 501

Often imitated, never matched, the 1947 Levi's 501xx is the gold standard of jeans. It's not just the button-fly or the slim-cut styling that makes this pair superior. They fit exquisitely well without the aid of high-tech body scans or computer-guided sewing machines. An icon from the moment they were introduced, 501s are coolly, subtly stylish in any shade of blue—from rich indigo to well-faded. Newer labels like Diesel, Rogan, and others have offered worthy competition, but nothing's come close to unseating 501s as the quintessential pair of jeans.

OPTIONS

BLUE

Blue straight-leg jeans are universally appealing.

DARK BLUE

Inky jeans are timeless. They're also the elegant pair you can dress up with a collared shirt and blazer.

FINISHES/WASHES

The wash of a jean speaks volumes about the man wearing it. Try wearing a pair of acid-wash jeans on your next date and you'll see what we mean. If you're going to experiment, stick with varying degrees of stone-wash. Otherwise, let your favorite pairs weather naturally.

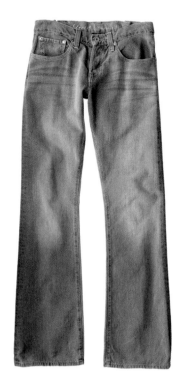

GRAY

Gray jeans, which have been having a moment in recent years, are destined to become a contemporary classic—especially when worn with a T-shirt and a black sweater.

WHITE

White jeans are the hardest style to pull off, but it's worth trying. Wear them with a simple, solid-colored sweater—and keep them spotless.

SLIGHT DISTRESS

Your choices in the gently distressed department are endless. But opt for subtle embellishment or you'll look like a Backstreet Boy.

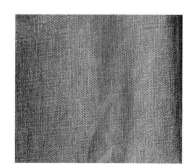

DON'T LET YOUR JEANS FALL BELOW YOUR HIPS. MAKE SURE THEY'RE SNUG ENOUGH TO STAY UP.

ROOMIER IS BETTER IN THE LEGS—FOR COMFORT AND LOOKS.

THE PERFECT FIT

There's actually no such thing as the perfect fit when it comes to jeans. Some men like to wear theirs a little baggy, while others—God bless 'em—prefer theirs on the tighter side. While both extremes can be taken entirely too far, there are plenty of options somewhere in the middle.

THE STRAIGHT

If you've got narrow hips and long legs, you'll do well with the standard straight leg, a classic, clean-cut *American Graffiti* look.

THE RELAXED

Relaxed-fit styles are the Everyman jeans (and essential for those with a taste for steak and Cabernet). Just be sure yours aren't too baggy, and secure them with a belt.

THE SKINNY

You don't have to be a member of The Strokes to wear skinny jeans, but opt for slim-cut only if you're lean and lanky.

KNOW YOUR BODY TYPE

Women's fashion magazines advise their readers about "Dressing for Your Body Type." Believe it or not, this applies to guys, too. Knowing your build and dressing accordingly is crucial with jeans. Be honest with yourself about your waist size. Those 501s from college probably haven't fit you in years.

If the 34 in one denim label doesn't fit you, try another. Jeans may have become a status symbol, but if the newest, most-hyped brand doesn't look right on you, stick with the classics.

Don't try to hide extra weight with baggy jeans. Aim for a pair cut to your personal taste—slightly snug or a little bit loose—and make sure it sits securely on your hips.

 Levi Strauss & Co. spent over $45,000 at a 2001 auction to buy back a pair of its own jeans, which were found in a Nevada mining town and dated to the 1880s.

DRESS UP, DRESS DOWN

How to wear one pair of jeans for three different occasions.

Jeans have range. They can be considerably dressed up or decidedly casual. If you're aiming for a formal look, select a pair of dark jeans and wear them with a crisp white shirt and patterned tie. Throw your navy blazer on top, add a white cotton pocket square, and you're dressed elegantly enough for a party.

If you're dressing for a laid-back evening, opt for jeans in a medium to dark wash and pair them with a collar shirt. Undo a button or two at the neck and roll up the sleeves. Trade the cap toes for loafers and skip the tie. If the occasion is a ballgame or a barbecue, you can wear a pair as faded as you like. Just make sure, as always, that your T-shirt is clean and your sneakers are spotless.

(A) FRIDAY MEETING
Thankfully casual Fridays are just about extinct. But if the work meeting is on the informal side, you can wear jeans with a blazer, tie, and polished wing tips.

(B) DRINKS AND DINNER
Shed the office-worthy blazer and tie and pair your jeans with a sweater instead.

(C) RUNNING ERRANDS
Throw on a polo and white tennis shoes for daytime shopping expeditions.

HOW TO PULL OFF

Jeans With a Shirt and Tie

Wearing jeans with the typical accompaniments for a suit—a shirt and tie—has officially become acceptable. And done right, it can be a stylish alternative to flannel trousers and a blazer. The golden rule: choose crisp, medium-to-dark jeans and save the faded pairs for T-shirts.

BEGINNER
Adopt a preppy, unfussy look in jeans, an oxford shirt, and a brightly colored tie.

INTERMEDIATE
Elevate the outfit to a slightly more formal level and add a cashmere crewneck or a blazer.

ADVANCED
If you pair dark indigo jeans with a white shirt, a black or navy tie, a blazer, and polished lace-ups, you're dressed for a dinner party.

DON'TS

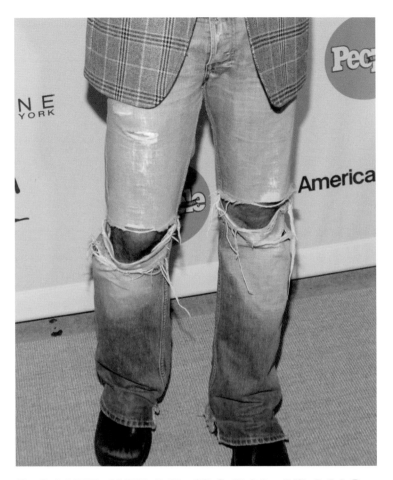

DON'T SWING LOW

"Dad jeans," the ones that sit just slightly below the ribcage, are bad. Low-rise jeans—and hip-huggers—the kind favored by Paris and Nicole—are far worse.

**DON'T WEAR
BOOT-CUT JEANS**

Jeans that flare at the ankle are suited to 12-year-old girls—not grown men.

DON'T WEAR TORN JEANS

If you want your jeans to demonstrate your affinity for hair bands or country stars, by all means, let it rip. Otherwise opt for intact, unadulterated denim.

HOW TO BUY

Don't obsess too much about finding that perfect faded look. While this has become something of a fixation for jeans junkies, the rest of us can rely on wear and tear to do the job.

DON'T GET SUCKED INTO TRENDS. STICK WITH THE CLASSICS AND YOU CAN'T GO WRONG.

WHEN YOU'RE IN THE DRESSING ROOM, BE SURE TO CHECK OUT YOUR ASS IN THE MIRROR. TOO SAGGY IS NO GOOD. WHILE YOU DO HAVE SOME WIGGLE ROOM IN THE FIT DEPARTMENT, THE JEANS SHOULDN'T HANG DOWN BELOW YOUR UNDERWEAR. YOU'RE PROBABLY GOING TO WEAR DENIM WITH A BLAZER AND WING TIPS— NOT A RAMONES T-SHIRT—SO BE PRACTICAL.

FINALLY, TAKE CARE OF YOUR JEANS. IT MAY SOUND SILLY, BUT COLOR CAN BE PRESERVED BY WASHING THEM INSIDE OUT. SOME GUYS GO SO FAR AS TO HAVE THEIR FAVORITE PAIRS DRY CLEANED. THIS IS DEFINITELY NOT A MUST, BUT IT'S NOT A CARDINAL SIN, EITHER, AS LONG AS YOU NEVER HAVE A SHARP CREASE PRESSED INTO YOUR JEANS.

RULES
OF STYLE

Tommy
Hilfiger

1 I love the classics. A great pair of old, old jeans, a white button-down shirt, a navy blazer, no socks, and Alden loafers.

2 For fall, I like gray flannel and the right dress shirt—shirts with double-button collars so they stand up on the neck. You can always tell the difference between an expensive dress shirt and an inexpensive one by the intensity of the color. For instance, the right light-blue shirt should be a deep light blue.

3 Men who are afraid to wear color are too conservative. There are certain men who work on Wall Street whose wives dress them. They'll buy a gray suit and a black, a navy, and a charcoal one. They'll wear a white or cream shirt every day with a red, yellow, or burgundy tie. And a black belt with black shoes. That to me is so boring. What about wearing orange with khaki?

4 Justin Timberlake has great style. He's a blend of American classic, hip-hop, and preppie.

5 I believe in "When in Rome…" In Nantucket, which is the epitome of American summer life, I'll wear Nantucket reds with a bright blazer. In Mustique, it's much more exotic, with Moroccan-inspired colors. And I also believe, when leaving Rome, take what's good about it and incorporate it into your life.

6 I like safari prints, especially for the home. But think of real authentic prints like you'd see in a safari lodge in Kenya—not zebra prints in hot-pink and blue.

7 If you go out in the city to a formal dinner, you need to dress appropriately. A gentleman should act like a gentleman and dress like one. He should war a navy suit with pinstripes, maybe a pink shirt with a white collar, and a navy-and-something tie. Women should dress sexy but sophisticated. There's nothing less attractive than a vampy woman wearing too little clothing, who's sticking out her chest and walking like a model when she's never been down a runway.

8 For black tie, men should dress properly in a tuxedo. No Nehru shirts with a diamond top button, hair all wet and slicked back, with a two-day beard. That's so L.A. Everyone looks dirty in L.A., walking around wearing the worst looking T-shirt they can find.

9 In the scope of the world, fashion isn't that important. It's entertainment, a luxury to enjoy. It's not a necessity. We could all get along very easily with the most basic basics.

CASUAL SHIRTS

CHAPTER 8

If your favorite T-shirt has an iron-on that reads "Iceman" there's a big chance that you need to rethink your approach to a certain wardrobe staple. You have more T-shirt options than you could possibly wear in a lifetime. Mass-market classics from brands like Hanes remain essentials, while top designers produce versions in luxurious cottons. Polo shirts no doubt take up ample real estate in your closet as well. We trust you wear them stylishly—not tucked into pleated khakis like a caddy on the PGA tour. The point is, you have a vast amount of choices when you go to put on a shirt. Those options don't involve a T-shirt bearing the words "The Dude Abides." Here's how to beef up your arsenal.

CASUAL SHIRT BASICS

(1) THE WHITE T-SHIRT

Every man needs a pile of freshly laundered, well-cut white T-shirts to call his own. Paired with the right items, tees are adaptable enough to be worn under a sport jacket or just with jeans or chinos. Reliable Hanes are good for layering under sweaters and collared shirts, but spring for finer-gauge varieties if you're going to wear the shirt solo.

(2) THE V-NECK

This variation on the classic tee is best limited to lounging around at home or at the beach. Pair with jeans or chinos.

(3) THE POLO

Not all polo shirts are created equal. The loose knit piqué cotton shirts first designed by tennis player René Lacoste back in 1929 have become a classic that's found favor with everyone from prepsters to rappers. Note: Unless you're Jay-Z, a loose shirt isn't a good look.

(4) THE HENLEY

Named after the shirts worn by the rowers of Henley-on-Thames in England, the modern version of the henley is a collarless top, usually of woven cotton, with buttons running down the chest. The henley can be worn with jeans or even dark trousers to an informal event as an alternative to the T-shirt. Avoid looking like a fop from an Evelyn Waugh novel by choosing one that's slim fitting and undoing the top couple of buttons.

(5) THE RUGBY

As anyone who's ever played the game of rugby can testify that the durability of the uniform is a natural wonder. Taken out of its sporting context, the rugby shirt is a fun, masculine top you can wear to Sunday brunch. The more you wear and wash it the better it gets, as the thick cotton breaks down and becomes more worn in. Rugby shirts work best in bold horizontal stripes, but don't go crazy—too many primary hues and you'll look like a presenter on *Playhouse Disney*.

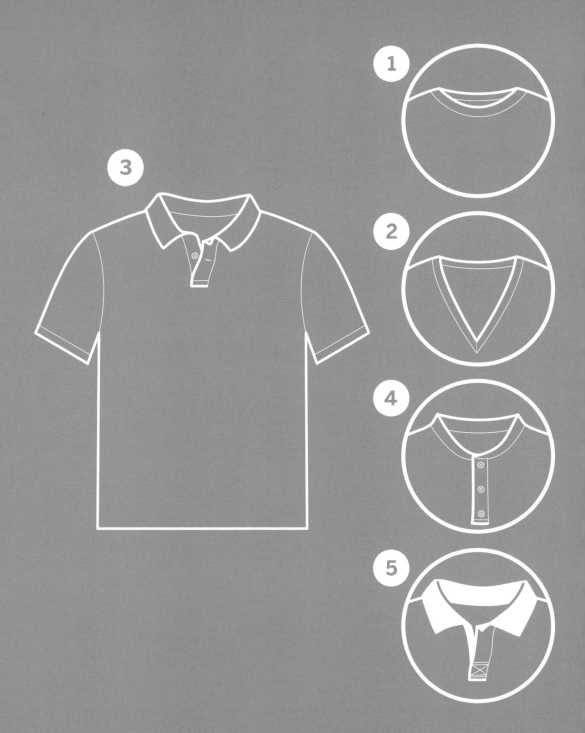

OPTIONS

SOLID COLOR T-SHIRT

Colored T-shirts punch up your casual wardrobe. Wear them alone or under a collared shirt with just a small triangle of color showing.

WHITE T-SHIRT

There is an ideal white T-shirt out there for every man. Look for it and when you find it, buy a dozen—just for starters.

RUGBY

The rugby has become a bona fide classic. You can use high-quality models as a stand-in for a polo shirt.

LONG-SLEEVE POLO

This under-appreciated polo makes a good stand-in for short-sleeve collared shirts when temperatures drop.

POLO

The polo is so ubiquitous that we forget what a classic it is. You can wear one—in any of the mind-boggling selection of colors—with almost anything.

STRIPED POLO

This is the classic golf shirt and it shouldn't be messed with. Wear it with chinos or under a blue blazer.

CONTRAST COLLAR POLO

Try a polo shirt with a collar in a contrasting hue as an alternative to styles in bold stripes and subdued solid colors.

V-NECK

V-neck shirts accentuate the chest so it helps to have the pecs to match. Make sure yours are fitted but not too tight.

HENLEY

A compromise between a T-shirt and a button-down, the henley is a weekend staple. Wear it untucked and always partially unbuttoned.

EVEN SHORT SLEEVES NEED TO FIT RIGHT—BUT THEY SHOULDN'T BE TOO TIGHT.

SHIRT SHOULD TOUCH YOUR BODY FROM SHOULDER TO WAIST WITHOUT BINDING.

THE PERFECT FIT

NOT TOO TIGHT

Skintight T-shirts say only one thing: meathead. Either cut back on the protein shakes or find a T-shirt that covers your body without hugging it.

· ·

NOT TOO LONG

A T-shirt that touches your knees is something your girlfriend wore when she was on grade-school sleepovers. Yours should be long enough to tuck in but it shouldn't hang below your hips.

POLOS

When choosing a polo, think of it as you would a regular shirt and figure out which style and brand works for your body shape and size—many of the leading brands have recently introduced slimmer silhouettes that look more modern. A word on the polo shirt collar: it was designed so that it could be turned up to block sunlight. But choose your moment—on the beach is appropriate, at a sales conference isn't. Be a turned-up collar user, not an abuser.

! Tennis champ **René Lacoste** invented the polo shirt in 1929 as a more comfortable alternative to the typical court attire of the time: a shirt and tie. **His nickname was "the Alligator," hence the logo.**

DRESS UP, DRESS DOWN

How to wear one polo shirt for three different occasions.

You can dress up a polo shirt for work by pairing it with a navy blazer, jeans, and a pair of loafers. The key is size: A too-big polo shirt will not—repeat, will not—work with a blazer and unless you're competing in the limbo competition on a Carnival Cruise liner, lose the shorts. Pants in light cotton or wool weaves will keep you cool without crossing the line to sloppy.

(A) **A DAY IN THE CITY**
Top a polo shirt with a blazer and add lace-ups instead of sneakers, and you can wear it to the Metropolitan Museum of Art.

B

TRAVELING

If you want to get comfortable on a plane, wear something soft but not too casual. A polo shirt tucked in and worn with a belt will get you straight from the jetway to a casual dinner.

C

A WEEKEND AWAY

This is a classic boating outfit, so what if you're not going near the water. Stay cool in loose cotton slacks and a bright polo.

HOW TO PULL OFF

A Blazer With Casual Shirts

The danger of pairing a casual shirt with a blazer can by summed up in two words: Sonny Crockett. The informality of the T-shirt should be complemented by a similar blazer—one in an unstructured fabric like cotton rather than a more formal wool. Don't roll up the sleeves.

BEGINNER

Avoid looking sloppy and wear a solid-color, graphics-free T-shirt—two layered on top of each other is even better—underneath a cotton blazer with jeans and clean white sneakers. Graphic tees are not an option.

INTERMEDIATE

Aim for a dressier look with a striped-cotton polo shirt—a button or two undone at the collar—worn with a woven belt and bucks or slightly worn-in lace-ups.

ADVANCED

If the shirt is a cashmere henley—with a white tee underneath—the jeans are dark, and the shoes are polished lace-ups, you can wear a blazer over a casual shirt to a dinner party.

DON'TS

DON'T TUCK A T-SHIRT INTO JEANS
You are not a 70-year-old veteran on his way to Costco for a jumbo pack of Tasty Beef Flavor Kibbles and Chunks.

DON'T ROLL
Do not roll up your sleeves to show off the hours you've spent pumping your biceps and triceps. Plain and simple, you will look like a chump.

DON'T WEAR T-SHIRTS WITH LOGOS OR SLOGANS

Leave the "Vote for Pedro" or "Do You Yahoo?" gimmicks to the people who've got nothing better to say. And your "I'm Only Two Girls Short of a Threesome" T-shirt? It's not doing you any favors.

HOW TO BUY

POLOS, HENLEYS, AND TEES ARE STAPLES LIKE JEANS ARE. WHEN YOU FIND A BRAND THAT SUITS YOU, BUY A BUNCH OF SHIRTS.

Throw your tees out when they're worn. Nothing says Homer Simpson more than a T-shirt you've been wearing since your glory days as a bartender.

NOT ALL COTTON IS CREATED EQUAL. MANUFACTURERS WILL ALERT YOU TO A BETTER GRADE OF COTTON— EGYPTIAN, SEA ISLAND, ETC.—BECAUSE THEY'LL NEED TO JUSTIFY THE GREATER PRICE OF THE SHIRT. IS IT WORTH THE MONEY? THE ANSWER DEPENDS ON YOU AND YOUR TASTE FOR LUXURY. (BUT, YES, IT IS.)

RULES
OF STYLE

Donna
Karan

1 Younger guys in New York—and most major cities around the world—are definitely cooler than the older, more established ones. There's nothing sexy about trying to be "established." Don't be threatened by power women. Lots of ladies are more independent these days, anyway. The less intimidated you are about that, the sexier you come across. I find men my age are too stiff. I can't go there anymore. I vibrate with a much younger energy. I'd definitely go out with a younger guy, there's not even a question in my mind.

2 There are fewer boundaries now between masculinity and femininity. It's not as controlled as it used to be. What used to be considered feminine is now sexy: Engage your creative side and let the women around you experience that. Tap into your senses of taste, smell, sight, and touch. It's sensual. Don't be afraid. Women are more attracted to aesthetically confident men. A creative man is just much more interesting, whether he's into art, or singing, or drama, or photography, or cooking, or writing. There's such a large platform to play with now. Women don't just want to sit there and watch football. I know I don't.

3 Take sexiness into account when you get dressed. There are no rules anymore. God knows I've dressed enough men to know. Why can't a man wear a skirt? Why does a man have to wear a tie with his suit? Don't. Casual is smarter and sexier. Once a man is stripped of his armor, he'll realized there's a great freedom to dressing. I like men who are dressed simply. To me a suit is not a suit—it's a jacket and pants. Only wear a tie if you have to, or randomly. A guy who's always in jeans and a sweater should occasionally put on a shirt and tie. That's when a tie is sexy—when it's a surprise. I like a man to look organic. Slick is out. Way out.

4 Men shouldn't have too many clothes. He should have a leather jacket, a black coat, a nice suit, some crisp shirts, a cool belt, and some old T-shirts.

5 Jeans are your most important piece of clothing, no question. They have to be worn. And they've got to be old. I also prefer that they be button-fly. The right jeans and a T-shirt can be sexier than the most expensive tailored suit.

6 I hate done hairdos. Never let it seem like you've spent too much time on your hair.

7 Frankly, I like bald. If you're losing your hair, don't get all freaked out. And definitely don't get plugs, no matter how much progress they've made. Go for it. Look at Ed Harris or Bruce Willis. Add a little hair to your face if you want. The best-looking guys in the world are Buddhist monks. They all shave their heads and they are gorgeous. So don't panic.

8 Shoes can really make or break a guy. I don't like flimsy little loafers. I like a man's shoe to have strength to it. Shoes tell a woman about the soul of a man—no pun intended. Nothing too shiny or too clunky.

SWEATERS

CHAPTER 9

As kids, we regarded sweaters as scratchy pieces of clothing our mothers insisted we carry with us when the weather forecast predicted a chill. As we grew up, they were what we grudgingly shrugged on instead of college sweatshirts when the occasion called for it. Now, knit pullovers and cardigans are an elementary part of our wardrobes and their function has become less important than their form. A slim crewneck adds the polish of a blazer to a shirt and tie. A cashmere cardigan can make a tailored jacket and a T-shirt elegant enough for a dinner party. You've learned to appreciate the sweater (and, of course, that Mom was right). Now make sure you're using it to its fullest potential.

SWEATER BASICS

STYLES

You've got options here. The roll neck, however, that holdover from your undergrad days, is not one of them. Vet the last from your closet if you haven't already.

(1) THE CREWNECK

A crewneck is, well, a crewneck, and a pullover with the classic neckline plays as well over a shirt and tie as it does over a white T-shirt. Just calibrate the material: A cotton crewneck will work with jeans and tees for a laid-back event; a cashmere one can go over a collared shirt to cocktails.

(2) THE V-NECK

There are regrettable V-neck sweaters—from aggressively preppy cream-colored cable-knits to ones that expose swaths of chest hair. Your collection should contain neither. Keep an arsenal of thin wool and cashmere pullovers with shallow V cuts to wear over collared shirts, with or without ties. Sweaters that have deep V-necks aren't taboo, just wear a fitted T-shirt underneath and take a look in the mirror before you leave the house to make sure you're not doing an inadvertent Burt Reynolds impression.

(3) THE TURTLENECK

The turtleneck category isn't as big a minefield as it seems. As long as you avoid bulk—not only in the cut, which should be slim, but in the material, which should be very lightweight and free of thick ribbing—and eye-popping colors, you can make the sweater a regular part of the rotation in fall and winter.

(4) THE CARDIGAN

Cardigans survived associations with grandpas and grunge to become a modern classic. A slim-fitting black or gray cashmere version can elevate jeans and a white T-shirt to cocktail-hour attire. Unless the look is deliberately fusty—an oversize nubby wool style meant for winter weekends, for example—yours should be snug and made from high-quality material.

(5) THE MATERIAL

If you're buying sweaters woven from top-quality wool and cashmere, you're probably hearing a lot about ply. Ply refers to the number of yarns used in the knitting—a higher ply means a heavier sweater, not a better quality one. Winter cashmere, for example, tends to be four to six ply, while the summer breed is usually no more than two ply. The bottom line: Look for 100 percent wool, cashmere, or cotton, and choose based on the season and how much layering you plan on doing. Cotton sweaters wear like another shirt layer. Wool adds warmth. Cashmere adds warmth with minimal thickness—and ultimately, it makes for the most versatile sweaters. You're not a snob to prefer it.

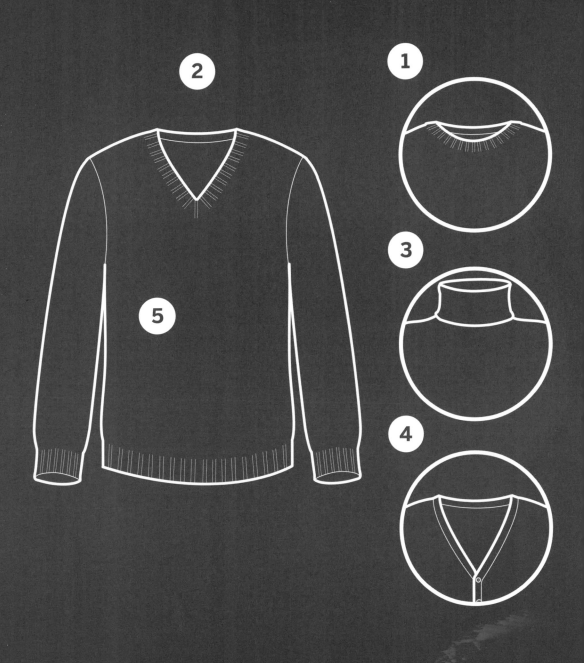

THE PERFECT SWEATER

A well-cut gray crewneck sweater is as essential to a man's wardrobe as a pair of everday jeans. A lightweight cashmere one that fits well can go under a suit to add warmth or over a T-shirt to make dark jeans appropriate for an evening out. Further argument for owning more than one: It's almost impossible for it to clash with anything else in your closet.

OPTIONS

CASHMERE

Soft cashmere sweaters provide warmth without bulk. Wear with flannel pants or under a jacket.

COTTON

Cotton sweaters often get overlooked, but they are perfect for cool summer evenings.

CREWNECK

Crewneck pullovers are winter staples. Liven them up with a little color and pair with dark jeans and classic dress shoes.

V-NECK

It's more stylish than a crewneck, but requires you to think about what you're going to wear under it before you throw it on.

FAIR ISLE
Some patterned sweaters should be reserved solely for the ski team, but the updated Fair Isle can be safely worn with faded jeans.

CABLE-KNIT
This textured sweater is as suited to the office as it is to the weekend. Pair with a shirt and a tie or wear with chinos.

WOOL
Sometimes a sweater is best used as an outer layer. Heavy wool provides warmth and comfort.

TURTLENECK
A turtleneck should be in every man's wardrobe. Wear one under a suit and with flat-front trousers.

CARDIGAN
A thin cardigan can lend the same polished look as a tailored jacket— with a lot more comfort.

FISHERMAN
The Irish fisherman's sweater is a classic utilitarian design. Make sure you wear it in a trimmer style.

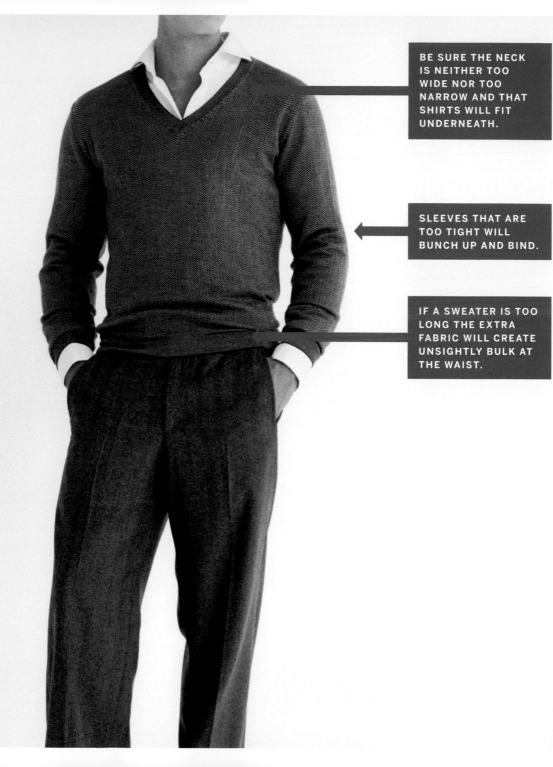

BE SURE THE NECK IS NEITHER TOO WIDE NOR TOO NARROW AND THAT SHIRTS WILL FIT UNDERNEATH.

SLEEVES THAT ARE TOO TIGHT WILL BUNCH UP AND BIND.

IF A SWEATER IS TOO LONG THE EXTRA FABRIC WILL CREATE UNSIGHTLY BULK AT THE WAIST.

THE PERFECT FIT

CLOSE TO THE BODY

With limited exceptions—certain styles of cardigans are supposed to be roomy—sweaters should be cut close to your body. Choose pullovers that are snug enough to be worn comfortably under a jacket but not so tight that you couldn't wear them over a collared shirt.

THE SHOULDERS

The best judge for whether a sweater fits you properly is the shoulders. Go down a size until the seam sits as close as possible to the center of each shoulder. Stop when the seam starts to creep toward your collarbone—and well before the hem of the sweater starts to creep up your torso.

THE BULK

A sweater that's bulky at the waist flatters no man (this is especially true with turtlenecks). A pullover should skim the sides of your torso but be long enough to cover your waistband.

! **The cardigan was named for the seventh Earl of Cardigan,** who gave his troops the knitted sweaters for extra warmth while they were fighting in the Crimean War in 1854.

DRESS UP, DRESS DOWN

How to wear one sweater for three different occasions.

(A) BASKETBALL GAME

A sweater and dark jeans are eveningwear, especially if the evening consists of standing up and cheering.

B **SUPERMARKET RUN**
Khakis and a sweater make errands easy work.

C **DRESSING FOR FALL**
To keep your layers from getting bunched up under a coat, wear a sweater instead of a jacket. You'll still be all business but you'll be warm.

HOW TO PULL OFF

A Sweater With a Suit

If you're going to wear a sweater under a suit, opt for a pullover, turtleneck, or cardigan in extra-thin merino wool or cashmere. A crewneck, a V-neck, or a vest in charcoal, black, or navy can make a shirt and tie look more put-together. Choose one that's solid-colored and cut close to the body, and wear it with a brightly patterned shirt and tie. If you end up shedding the suit jacket, you'll still look polished.

BEGINNER

Neutral sweaters as an added layer are the place to start. Gray is the safest. But navy blue and black will work well too.

INTERMEDIATE

Start adding colors. Believe it or not, red can act as a neutral especially with a dark-gray or navy-blue suit. But lavender and brown work well with many shirt-and-tie combos.

ADVANCED

Patterned sweaters and sweater vests will spice up your existing wardrobe. Big patterns like argyle work well on sweaters and stripes and herringbones work well too.

DON'TS

DON'T WEAR THE CHRISTMAS SWEATER

No article of clothing in your closet should be pegged to a holiday. The only excuses for wearing a "festive" sweater: You're a kindergarten teacher, you're a kids TV presenter, or your grandmother gave it to you—and you're at her house.

DON'T WEAR THE SKI SWEATER

An alpine-inspired sweater can be stylish—think a small-scale wintry print worn with jeans on the weekends—but an oversize, chunky-knit sweater bearing reindeers isn't appropriate anywhere off the slopes, or on them either.

DON'T WEAR THE COSBY SWEATER

Bill Cosby's sweaters are the butt of jokes for a reason. By all means, experiment with sweaters in brightly colored stripes—preferably lean-cut crewnecks—but steer clear of any pattern so loud you wouldn't wear it to work. And never wear a printed sweater with anything but solid-colored shirts and trousers.

HOW TO BUY

A TOP-SHELF SWEATER IS WELL WORTH THE INVESTMENT. IT WILL PILL LESS, HOLD ITS SHAPE LONGER, AND FIT BETTER THAN CHEAPER-MADE VARIETIES. THAT DOESN'T MEAN ALL OF YOUR SWEATERS HAVE TO BE CASHMERE—MERINO WOOL OR A FINER QUALITY SHEEP'S WOOL ARE WORTHY MATERIALS—BUT IT'S WORTH SPRINGING FOR PRICEY KNITS. PLUS, MANUFACTURERS ARE FINDING NEW WAYS TO MAKE CASHMERE SWEATERS MORE AFFORDABLE, SO YOU NO LONGER HAVE TO BE A HILTON TO SWING A GOOD-SIZE COLLECTION OF THEM.

Consider the season when choosing your sweaters. Cotton and lightweight cashmere are ideal for spring and summer. Wool and higher-ply cashmere are best for colder months.

BE SURE TO PROTECT YOUR SWEATERS, ESPECIALLY THE CASHMERE ONES—HAVE THEM DRY CLEANED AT A PLACE YOU TRUST.

THE MOVIES THAT SHAPED MEN'S STYLE

SOPHISTICATED

The Philadelphia Story (1940)
Falcon (1941)
Casablanca (1942)
The Man in the Gray Flannel Suit (1956)
Funny Face (1957)
Vertigo (1958)
North by Northwest (1959)
Ocean's 11 (1960)
Breakfast at Tiffany's (1961)
Charade (1963)
The Thomas Crown Affair (1968)
The Great Gatsby (1974)
American Gigolo (1980)
The Untouchables (1987)
Wall Street (1987)
Gattaca (1997)

CASUALLY CHIC

La Dolce Vita (1960)
The Graduate (1967)
Bonnie & Clyde (1967)
Love Story (1970)
Shampoo (1975)
Ferris Bueller's Day Off (1986)
The Talented Mr. Ripley (1999)

COOL

Alfie (1966)
Fast Times at Ridgemont High (1982)
Risky Business (1983)
Do the Right Thing (1989)
Reservoir Dogs (1992)
Pulp Fiction (1994)
Men in Black (1997)
The Matrix (1999)

ADVENTUROUS

Out of Africa (1985)
Top Gun (1986)
Full Metal Jacket (1987)

REBELLIOUS

A Streetcar Named Desire (1951)
On the Waterfront (1954)
Rebel Without a Cause (1955)
The Good, The Bad, and The Ugly (1966)
Bullitt (1968)
Midnight Cowboy (1969)
Zabriskie Point (1970)
Tommy (1975)
Taxi Driver (1976)
The Outsiders (1983)
Desperado (1995)
Gangster No. 1 (2000)

ECCENTRIC

A Clockwork Orange (1971)
Blade Runner (1982)
Dick Tracy (1990)
Pirates of the Caribbean (2003)

TREND-SETTING

Blow Up (1966)
Saturday Night Fever (1977)
Quadrophenia (1979)
The Hunger (1997)
Velvet Goldmine (1998)

GRUNGE

My Own Private Idaho (1991)
Singles (1992)
Reality Bites (1994)

RULES
OF STYLE

Christopher Bailey

Creative Director, Burberry

1 | If your jewelry or cuff links are the first thing somebody comments on when they look at you, they're probably a little too much. A watch should be discreet, not opulent. It should go with everything.

2 | It's fun to wear things that are "of the moment." Just not everything. That's too much.

3 | You need to sense the body underneath the clothes. When you can't see the body underneath the clothing, it looks sloppy.

4 | **If you're somebody who's not so into fashion, just dress for the environment that you're in.** If you're in the city, stick with clothing that's dark and tailored.

5 | I really admire men who can wear ties. I love the idea of it, but men my age don't feel comfortable in a suit. I feel like such a prick in one, like I'm pretending to be the big guy here. And I'm really sick of that suit-with-sneakers-and-T-shirt look. The shoes are key. I hate when you see someone in tailored pants and brand-new sneakers and you can just tell it's so not their personality. I want to tell them to get a nice pair of brogues.

6 | A suit needs a nice classic shirt. Opulent prints and bright colors are better with jeans and chinos than suits.

7 | I think guys are definitely less intimidated by the whole concept of grooming in the last few years, but it has nothing to do with those five guys [from *Queer Eye for the Straight Guy*]. It has more to do with poeple like David Beckham, a straight guy brave enough to go out in a skirt or pluck his eyebrows. And he's the most masculine soccer player, married to this beautiful woman. That's more influential than those five guys.

8 | A few little squirts of fragrance on your chest is better than ten squirts on your neck. And unless you're really, really handsome, don't get highlights.

9 | **If you feel a little bit overdressed, you're probably really overdressed.**

10 | You have to be a certain type to carry off a leather jacket. If you do wear one, it should be tailored. A boxy one will age you.

11 | When it comes to dressing, I think men have to try a little harder, a little less hard as well. It's contradictory, but I think we're lazy. You have to be a little adventurous, but you have to listen to your soul and have good instincts. You know if you look like a dick. You have mirrors.

OUTERWEAR

CHAPTER 10

Nothing can ruin the right outfit faster than the wrong coat. You could be wearing the most luxurious, perfectly fitted, cashmere bespoke suit, but if your raincoat is ragtag and faded or your overcoat is half a size too big, you look no more stylish than a flasher. Lest we forget, first impressions can be everything—make sure your outer layer represents you well.

OUTERWEAR BASICS

(1) THE MATERIAL

Odds are you'll get the most use out of an overcoat made from either wool or cashmere. Alpaca and camel hair are fine alternatives to cashmere, but nothing looks or feels as good as a cashmere overcoat; it adds warmth without bulk, keeping your silhouette sleek.

(2) BREAST POCKET

Some overcoats have a breast pocket that was originally designed to accommodate a colorful silk handkerchief or a pair of thin driving gloves. If your coat does come with one, we recommend keeping it empty.

(3) SINGLE-BREASTED VERSUS DOUBLE-BREASTED

Single- or double-breasted is as always, a matter of preference, but double-breasted overcoats won't cover your chest, leaving you wide open on cold mornings. The lapels should be slim and the collar should be flipped up only when the weather calls for it.

(4) ONE IS NOT ENOUGH

Think about getting more than one overcoat. You'll probably need a lighter weight coat either for the rain or for those in-between seasons where you need a top-coat but a real overcoat will be too warm.

SCARVES? GO TO PAGE 234

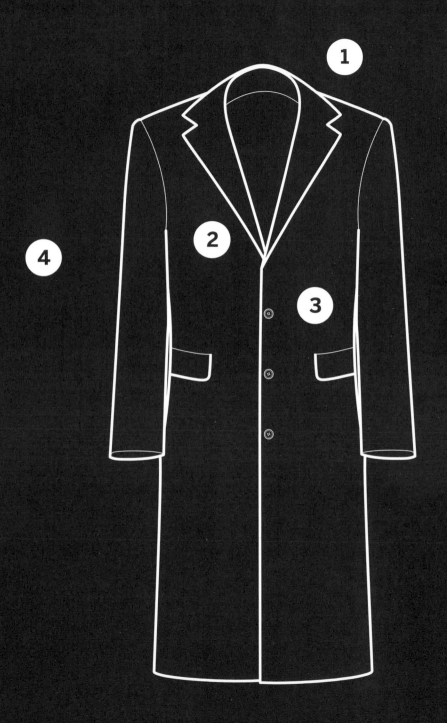

THE PERFECT OVERCOAT

The true mark of the perfect overcoat is when you don't want to take it off indoors. A single-breasted, cashmere overcoat can give you just the right dose of elegance, whether you're wearing it with jeans and a sweater or a sleek, peak-lapel tuxedo. You'll know you've slipped into this coat the moment you put it on. You'll linger in front of the mirror for an extra few beats before leaving the house and, ultimately, you'll take your time peeling it off once you reach your destination. And while you look as good as you feel in a cashmere overcoat, you must resist the temptation to wear it indoors so others can catch a glimpse.

OPTIONS

PARKA

High-performance jackets help you weather severe storms. Even if you're just trekking to Starbucks.

DOWN JACKET

The down jacket is back from the dead. Opt for the newer slimmed-down versions and you'll avoid any comparisons to the Michelin Man.

CHESTERFIELD COAT

An overcoat cut slim with a hem that hits the knee will keep you warm without weighing you down.

CAMEL-HAIR COAT

Polished and masculine, the camel overcoat complements everything from suits to courduroys.

PEACOAT

The peacoat now comes in a variety of colors and fabrics. Stick with lean, shoulder-hugging versions in classic blue, gray, or black.

DENIM JACKET

Jean jackets have reached icon status in part because of their versatility. You can even wear one with a shirt and tie.

MILITARY JACKET

Military style has applied to coats since men rode horses into battle. Army-inspired jackets are as stylish as they are utilitarian.

BARBOUR JACKET

When a parka is too casual and a camel coat too formal, the functional and classic Barbour jacket steps in.

TRENCH COAT

Another military design adapted to civilian use: The trench handles the cold as well as the wet.

MACINTOSH

If the weather report says rainy but warm, the Mac is indispensable.

TOGGLE COAT

A collegiate staple, the toggle coat—without the hood—can be grown-up. Use this casual overcoat to smarten up weekend looks.

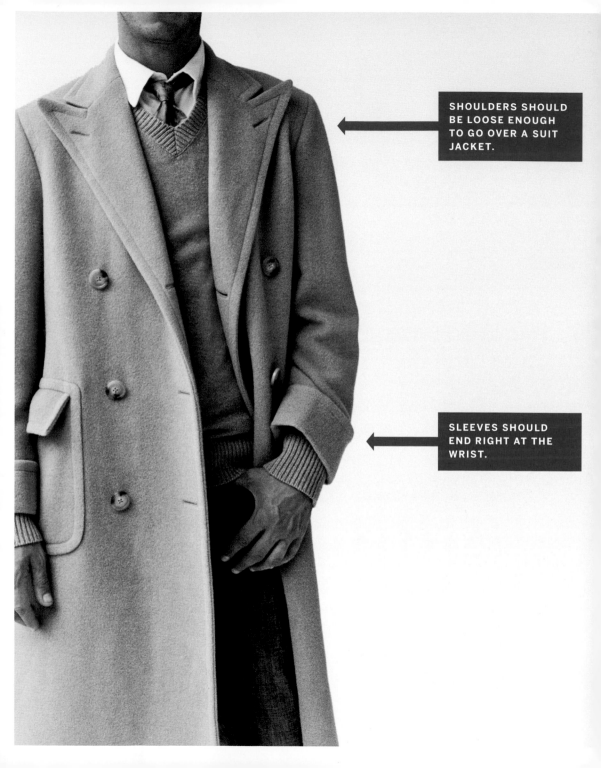

SHOULDERS SHOULD BE LOOSE ENOUGH TO GO OVER A SUIT JACKET.

SLEEVES SHOULD END RIGHT AT THE WRIST.

THE PERFECT FIT

Overcoats

NO BULK

Your overcoat needs to fit over the rest of what you are wearing, but it shouldn't be too roomy. That means it should not fit like a blanket or a poncho. It should accommodate a suit but still show your form when buttoned.

....

THE LENGTH

You can find a wide range of overcoats in many lengths. Some are three-quarter and will cover your suit jacket but not go down as far as your knees. These are a little more casual but help get you through the average day.

....

THE BELT

A belt is best used on a classic trench. It gives the coat a waist and breaks up the long run of fabric on taller men.

! **Thomas Burberry invented the trench coat in 1895 as a raincoat for British army officers.** It was made of gabardine—a fabric Burberry also created.

Jackets

THE SLEEVES

Figure out what you're going to wear the jacket with. Over a suit or sport jacket, you don't want the jacket to ride up on the sleeves. Nor do you want the jacket's sleeves to droop down over your fingertips. And don't even think about rolling the sleeves back into cuffs.

THE LENGTH

A three-quarter length coat should hit about mid-thigh. A shorter jacket—a denim or corduroy style, for example—should hit no higher than the waist.

THE POCKETS

Exterior pockets can be bulky and overly complicate the appearance of a shorter coat. If you have height and heft, that's not a problem, but a smaller guy is going to look overloaded with big pockets bulging out of the front of his coat.

! **The black leather jacket** beame a symbol of youthful rebellion when Marlon Brando wore a Perfecto One Star as Johnny Strabler in the 1954 film *The Wild One.*

DRESS UP, DRESS DOWN

How to wear one overcoat for three different occasions.

Overcoats are inherently versatile. They're meant to cover what's underneath, not blend with it. So you can drape the coat over your shoulders and see the suit beneath; add a scarf and hat; or wear a textured coat, like a corduroy or denim jacket, to make your whole look more casual.

(A) **THURSDAY NIGHT DINNER**
If you're en route from the office to a dinner out with friends, throw a charcoal overcoat on over your suit and loosen up the look with a chunky knit scarf and a complementary hat.

B AFTERNOON SOCCER GAME

Elegant as it is, an overcoat can easily be dressed down. Wear it over a washed-cotton shirt and a sweater with jeans and sneakers to an afternoon soccer game.

C NEIGHBORHOOD LUNCH

If the occasion is somewhat informal—like lunching with neighbors—layer your overcoat over a denim jacket and wool or cotton pants and accessorize with a dark knit scarf.

HOW TO PULL OFF

The Denim Jacket

The denim jacket is so universal, you'd think it would be difficult to screw it up. It isn't. Men wear the classic layer in the wrong color, cut, and context all the time. Follow these guidelines and you won't make that mistake.

● ● ○

BEGINNER

First off, don't wear a denim jacket with jeans. It bears repeating. Do wear a slim-cut basic style with flat-front trousers and T-shirts. Reserve this look for outside the office only.

● ● ○

INTERMEDIATE

Try a jean jacket cut from corduroy or canvas. You'll get the same styling with a more versatile texture and match-friendly fabric. This you *can* wear with jeans.

● ● ●

ADVANCED

Slip a narrowly tailored, undistressed denim jacket on under a corduroy blazer or a lightweight overcoat. The layer will add welcome texture.

DON'TS

DON'T WEAR AN OUTER LAYER THAT IS SHORTER THAN YOUR INNER LAYER

This goes especially for wearing ski jackets with suits. The two concepts don't mix and you will create visual confusion for everyone who comes into contact with you.

DON'T WEAR LEATHER BOMBER JACKETS. JUST DON'T.

HOW TO BUY

LOOK FOR FABRICS THAT ARE EASY TO CARE FOR AND RESISTANT TO STAINS. PATTERNS WORK WELL FOR HIDING LIFE'S LITTLE DISAPPOINTMENTS.

Think of a coat as an investment. It's something you'll want to own for a long time. Avoid the bright or trendy hues that you'll regret when you find your only way of keeping warm makes you look like a holdover from a decade ago.

GET A GOOD TAILOR TO ADJUST A PRICEY OVERCOAT FOR YOU. HAVE HIM MAKE SURE THE BACK FITS PROPERLY AND THE SLEEVES COVER YOUR SUIT JACKET OR BLAZER SLEEVES.

YOUR COAT IS THE FIRST ITEM OF CLOTHING THAT PEOPLE SEE. IT'S WORTH SPLURGING.

RULES OF STYLE

Zac Posen

1 | **You have to be taller than five feet eight to wear a double-breasted jacket.** If you're not, you can look very square. You get into sea-captain territory. If you're not tall, you should go for a shorter, one-button jacket.

2 | **You should always carry a handkerchief.** It's a courteous thing to have. If I'm out at night, I keep a handkerchief on hand for a lady.

3 | **Loro Piana's linen shirts are a great thing to have.** They're soft and comfortable. And they have a wonderful crispness to them if you keep them ironed.

4 | **Scents that are soapy and sweet don't work on men.** Orange blossom is the sweetest fragrance a man should wear—and it's really refreshing.

5 | **Beautiful pajamas are essential.** The best are Sea Island-cotton plaid ones from Turnbull & Asser.

6 | **I like long hair on men with straight hair, but I'm not ready for ponytails again.** And a messed-up Beatles bob is cute but should probably not be worn by anyone over the age of 35.

7 | **Shoes are such an important element of style.** I mostly wear an Yves Saint Laurent Johnny boot. I almost never wear sneakers. I have a pet peeve about sneakers with evening dress. There was a moment when all the men in the fashion industry started wearing them out at night. It drove me nuts.

8 | **I'm not crazy about backpacks with suits.** My boyfriend used to carry one every day, so I bought him an Hermés briefcase to use instead.

9 | **Sean Combs can wear absolutely anything and so can André Leon Talley.** They take risks and they enjoy it. Their enjoyment is why they're able to wear what they do. There's no discomfort.

10 | **I love turtlenecks, but knit turtlenecks, not jersey.** Never jersey.

UNDERWEAR

CHAPTER 11

It's no longer the case that men have two basic choices—boxers or briefs—when it comes to underwear. Developments in design and materials mean that we're faced with ever more complicated and—thankfully—comfortable options. Whatever your preference, one rule remains: If your underwear has the words girl bait printed on the front you're not getting out enough.

OPTIONS

FLANNEL PAJAMAS

While cotton should be the default option for pajamas, cold winter nights call for the warmth of flannel.

UNDERSHIRT

Buy your basic white undershirts in bulk for winter warmth. Always wear beneath a shirt unless you work for Tony Soprano.

BRIEFS

Whether you wear them every day or just for the gym, these are your best bet for support.

BOXERS

Whatever you're packing, you'll have more freedom in a pair of boxers.

BOXER BRIEFS

Boxer briefs offer the support of traditional briefs with the roomier fit of boxers.

ATHLETIC SOCKS

A thicker sock gives you the cushioning you need when running or playing ball.

DRESS SOCKS

Keep a drawer full of cotton blend socks in basic colors. When they're threadbare toss them, never wear them.

THE PERFECT FIT

THE CHOICES
You're either a boxers guy or a briefs guy. That's all there is to it. Unless, that is, if you're a a boxer briefs guy.

....

THE LONG JOHN
If you're spending time outdoors when the mercury dips, a pair of thermal long johns under pants or jeans will keep you from suffering winter chills.

....

THE FABRIC
Whatever fit or design you choose, whether it's from a designer or a department store, invest in as high a quality cotton as you can afford.

! **Boxer briefs** officially broke out when Calvin Klein featured them in a 1993 ad starring Marky Mark.

HOW TO PULL OFF

Colorful Socks

Wearing brightly colored socks is a look championed by Italians and British men who like to indulge their peacock tendencies a little more than American men do. Don't let that put you off: Stripes, dots, argyles, and checks—or just plain color—can make a bold statement. Done badly, however it can make you look like a chump.

Bear the following in mind: Socks are a transition from the pants to the shoe. Try to keep one color constant or blend the two colors being brought together. When in doubt, lean toward the color of the pants.

Think about the shirt and tie you are wearing. If you pick up colors from the shirt and tie, your socks will blend seamlessly into the same outfit.

BEGINNER
Transition from blue, gray, and black by wearing socks in subtle patterns or lighter blues and browns. They'll match the clothes you already have.

INTERMEDIATE
While you might not want to go the whole hog, try red socks with jeans and brown shoes.

ADVANCED
Stripes, patterned, and clocked socks are for style connoisseurs only. Apply similar rules as the ones for shirts and ties—match colors and balance scale.

DON'TS

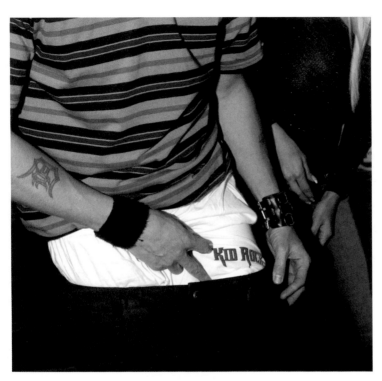

DON'T GET TOO CUTE WITH YOUR UNDERWEAR

Just because your underwear is seen by a select few doesn't mean that you shouldn't treat it with the same degree of seriousness you would a shirt. Lose the thong and the tighty-whities with the iron-on Tweetie bird.

DON'T WEAR TANK TOPS AS SHIRTS

Even if you've spent the winter pumping iron, limit the sleeveless look to the beach and the wrestling ring.

DON'T EXPOSE YOUR UNDERWEAR

Unless you attach the suffix *izzle* to every other word, revealing your skivvies isn't a good look.

HOW TO BUY

FIND THE STYLE AND BRAND THAT WORKS BEST FOR YOU AND STOCK UP. UNDERWEAR TAKES A POUNDING (NO PUN INTENDED) SO MAKE SURE TO REPLACE WORN VERSIONS REGULARLY.

Throw your undershirts, underpants, and socks out as soon as they start showing serious wear. That hole won't go away, and, one day, it's going to cause you some embarrassment.

THINK LIKE AN ARMY QUARTERMASTER: HAVE SPARE SOCKS, UNDERSHIRTS, AND BRIEFS READY TO REPLACE WORN VERSIONS.

RULES OF STYLE

Kenneth Cole

1 | **Years ago, we all wore the same gray suits and white shirts.** On weekends, we wore torn jeans and T-shirts. It's like we all showed up at a costume party wearing the same costume. Now we all spend a lot of time getting dressed in the morning to make it look like we don't care.

2 | **Every man should own a navy blazer.** It's refined and functional, like a modern-day briefcase that holds your phone, iPod, wallet, and notes.

3 | **I'm not into hats unless they have a purpose.** Unless it's hard and you're rappelling down a mountain, I don't want to see it.

4 | **I've always designed my shoes with rubber soles because they're comfortable.** I believe you should be able to walk in your shoes.

5 | **You should always wear something that's tailored.** If you want to wear jeans, wear them with a button-down. Don't put on a big, heavy sweater.

6 | **Getting dressed in the morning is a self-fulfilling reality.** If you don't look good, you don't feel good, and you might as well go and get hit by a bus.

7 | **I like straight-leg jeans with boots.** Boots hide imperfections, so your jeans can be a little long or short, and it won't matter.

8 | **Belts are great accessories.** They're modern-day holsters. But the bigger they are, the less practical they are. And I like practical.

9 | **I'm not a big fan of tuxes.** I haven't worn one in years. I'll go to work in a black blazer and jeans and then switch to black pants and a straight tie before I go out.

10 | **Some individuals think clothes are creative artistic expression, but they end up getting in their own way.** Like Michael Moore—I'd love to do a makeover on him.

SHOES

Your footwear options got infinitely more interesting in the last decade. Custom-made wing tips became collector's items. Reissues of vintage sneakers gained cult followings. Mandals were hotly debated. While that doesn't mean your interest in what you wear below the ankle needs to rival an oenophile's fascination with wine, you should probably know more than how to keep your cap toes shined.

SHOE BASICS

① THE LACES

The rules for men's footwear may be less stringent, but it is an inescapable fact that a lace-up still looks better with a suit than a slip-on. The general rule is that the more eyelets the shoe has the more formal it is. Classic cap toes and wing tips should have at least five.

② THE COLOR

Black will always be dressier than brown. If you're suiting up for a board meeting or a formal event, go with the former. If necessary, however, you can pair brown lace-ups with suits—especially navy or charcoal—as long as they're scuff-free.

③ THE MATERIAL

Glossy leather is the fail-safe choice, but you should feel free to experiment with suede—starting with a pair of classic bucks and progressing to exotic materials like alligator and ostrich or the growing number of antiqued leathers. Note: Battered isn't the same as distressed.

④ THE TOE

An elongated toe is unequivocally classier than a square. That doesn't mean all your lace-ups should be pointy—lots of elegant cap toes have squared-off tips—but unless you're aiming for mid-nineties nostalgia, no shoes you wear should have a blunt, squared-off toe.

⑤ THE WELT

Well-made lace-ups should have a close welt—the seam where the upper meets the sole and creates the outer edge of the shoe. It should be visible, but it shouldn't extend so far past the edge of the shoe that it creates a ledge.

⑥ THE SOLE

A thin sole is the hallmark of a cheap shoe—plus, it not only looks cut-rate, it wears out more quickly. Yours should be at least a quarter-of-an-inch thick and preferably leather, not rubber.

⑦ THE BROGUING

Traditionalists will tell you that the more broguing—decorative stitching and perforated and serrated edges—a shoe has, the less dressy it is. But while it's true that heavily embellished bucks look better with sport jackets and tweed than with pinstripe suits, this rule is flexible.

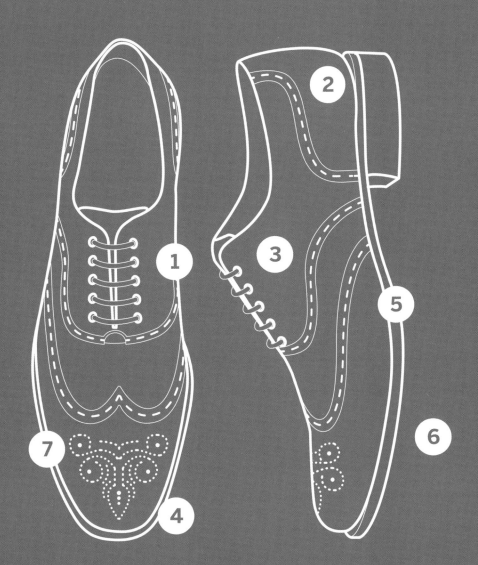

OPTIONS

LOAFERS
The loafer has moved beyond its preppy roots. Wear this basic with any casual look involving jeans or trousers.

OXFORDS
A good pair of oxfords are the cornerstone of a stylish wardrobe. Remember to keep them polished and to steer clear of puddles.

ANKLE BOOTS
Ankle boots are refined enough to wear well with both tailored and casual trousers.

SANDALS
Let your feet breath in the summer. Sandals go well with soft linen or cotton fabrics, but make sure they are made of leather.

MONK-STRAPS

An elegant alternative to loafers, this slip-on is almost universally flattering.

SPECTATORS

Spectators—cream-colored shoes with brown or black accents—are not for everyone, but they can be very stylish when worn correctly.

WING TIPS

Wing-tip shoes add flair to the serious business look. And yes, only wear them with suits—they're too formal for khakis or jeans.

FLIP-FLOPS

No matter how popular flip-flops become as a summer staple you should only wear yours at the beach or the pool.

WORK BOOTS

The classic work boot protects you from slushy sidewalks and arctic chills.

DRIVING SHOES

The driving moc was invented to let you feel a car's pedals better. Now it's an alternative to wearing slippers in public.

THE PERFECT FIT

THE RIGHT SIZE

Shoes are a fashion item. So it's easy to get distracted by chiseled toes or points instead of paying attention to boring details like size and—more importantly—the width of your foot. Your feet are not the exact same size, so, unless you want to go the whole hog at a custom shoemaker, you need a strategy.

Think of shoes the same way you think of suits. Find one or two manufacturers with fits that suit your feet. You can even see if they'll order you a specific pair if your feet are especially wide or narrow.

MADE-TO-MEASURE

If you've graduated to custom-made suits and shirts, made-to-measure shoes aren't an extravagance. A pair of cobbler-crafted shoes will feel better, look better, and last longer than the mass-produced breed. Start by honing in on a shoemaker whose style suits the shape of your feet. Find a pair or two you like and have them calibrated to your feet and made in a couple of different materials.

! **Over 90 percent** of people have feet that are mismatched sizes.

Sneakers

Sneakers are a fashion staple and a lifestyle statement. Whether high tops, slip-ons, or high-tech cross trainers, your choice in footwear says volumes, so choose wisely.

The perfect pair of sneakers is as crucial to a well-balanced wardrobe as elegant lace-ups are. These aren't utilitarian running shoes or bulky versions made for playing ball, but sneakers that up an outfit's style quotient. These shoes—a pristine pair of Stan Smiths or Jack Purcells, for example—are the ones you wear with dark jeans and collared shirts, or even with wool trousers and crewneck sweaters. They toe the line between casual and conservative like no other accessory does. Find the ones you love, buy two pairs, and spring for new ones when they get dingy. It won't take you long to wear them out.

! **Sixty percent** of people in the United States have worn **Converse's Chuck Taylors** in their lifetime.

EVOLUTION OF THE SNEAKER

After studying chicken feet, William J. Riley creates his New Balance prototypes.

Champion badminton player Jack Purcell designs a dependable court shoe for Converse that will eventually become a classic.

Bill Bowerman and Phil Knight each contribute $500 to start up Blue Ribbon Sports, which will eventually become Nike.

1916   **1923**   **1936**   **1971**

1906   **1935**   **1964**

U.S. Rubber Company launches Keds. The shoe's rubber soles spark an advertising agency to call them "sneakers" because they were quiet.

Chuck Taylor becomes the first basketball player to endorse a pair of sneakers, putting his signature on Converse All Stars.

Jesse Owens wins four gold medals at the Berlin Olympic Games wearing shoes made by the German Dassler brothers, who will later form PUMA and Adidas.

Bill Bowerman, head track coach at the University of Oregon, pours rubber into a waffle iron to create a lighter sole—the basis for Nike sneakers.

RUN DMC releases the album *Raising Hell*, which features the song "My Adidas." Darryl "D.M.C." McDaniels often wore his Adidas without laces and with the tongues flapping. This begins a symbiotic relationship between hip-hop music and footwear.

Sean Penn, as Jeff Spicoli, popularizes Vans slip-ons in *Fast Times at Ridgemont High*.

Nike Air Force 1 25th anniversary edition of crocodile-skin shoes is released.

PUMA debuts the limited edition Top Winner Thrift, 510 pairs of one-of-a-kind shoes created from vintage clothing.

1982   **1985**   **1991**   **2000**   **2005**

1981   **1986**   **2002**   **2007**

Japanese shoe designer, Onitsuka Tiger, creates a shoe specifically for the competitive sport of Tug of War.

Nike signs Michael Jordan to an endorsement deal. That same year, the first pair of Air Jordans are released, the beginning of a series that's still being issued.

Dee Brown bends down to pump up his Reebok Pump shoes before performing his winning "no-look" dunk during the NBA All Star Slam Dunk Contest.

Adidas introduces the first sneaker with a built-in microprocessor.

The sneakers Wilt Chamberlain wore when he broke a NBA record sell at Sotheby's for $55,000.

HOW TO PULL OFF

White Shoes

Wearing white shoes is an art form—one well worth perfecting. Two tips: Invest in leather cleaner and avoid shiny white shoes.

BEGINNER
White-shoe novices should start with a pair of alabaster bucks. Pair them with jeans and a collared shirt and complement them with striped socks in colors like navy and pink—or better yet, none.

INTERMEDIATE
White-leather brogues are slightly less subtle than bucks. Try a pair of creamy leather wing tips and wear them with jeans and a blazer.

ADVANCED
Once you're comfortable with white shoes, graduate to a pair of spectators. Wear them in the summer, with light-colored pants and a tailored shirt.

DON'TS

**DON'T WEAR
SQUARE-TOE SHOES**
These shoes had a moment 10
years ago. They were unstylish
then, they are unstylish now.

DON'T WEAR FLIP-FLOPS WITH SUITS

Or with any other pants for that matter. Flip-flops are great
for the beach. They're great for the pool. You can even wear
them in the shower, if you like. But they don't belong on
the street, in the office, or anywhere else miles from shore.

HOW TO BUY

BUY THE WRONG SHOES AND YOU'LL REGRET IT. NOT ONLY WILL THEY BE UNCOMFORTABLE BUT THEY COULD ALSO DAMAGE YOUR FEET. FIRST, HAVE YOUR FEET MEASURED. YOU MIGHT THINK YOU KNOW WHAT SIZE YOU ARE, BUT THERE'S A CHANCE YOU COULD BE WRONG. SECOND, WHEN YOU FIND A STYLE YOU LIKE AND YOU'VE TRIED THEM ON, TAKE A WALK AROUND THE STORE. ONLY THEN WILL YOU GET SENSE OF HOW GOOD A FIT THEY ARE.

REMEMBER THAT SHOES NEED REST AND RECOVERY. BUY SEVERAL PAIRS AND ROTATE THEM. ALWAYS WIPE OFF SALT IN THE WINTER AND GET A REGULAR SHINE.

Shop around. Every manufacturer has a different fit. Find a brand you like and buy a few pairs in different styles.

WHEN YOU'RE NOT WEARING YOUR SHOES ALWAYS PLACE SHOE TREES INSIDE THEM. CEDAR ONES ARE BEST AS THEY ABSORB MOISTURE AS WELL AS MAINTAIN THE SHAPE OF YOUR FOOTWEAR.

RULES
OF STYLE

Donatella
Versace

1 | **A man looks best in well-tailored pants with a low waist and a T-shirt.** For this winter, a camel coat. To dress up, pinstripe suits with dark shirts.

2 | **Bill Clinton is fascinating, always perfectly dressed.** He's glamorous—the way he talks, the way he walks.

3 | **Middle-aged men should not wear black leather jackets.** They belong to rock and roll and young kids.

4 | **Ben Affleck looks like a nice American boy.** He's a gorgeous man, but he should have more attitude, be more dangerous.

5 | **Jewelry is okay if a man knows how to wear it.** But if he's wearing a blue suit and then tries to add jewelry, it doesn't work. I don't like men bastardized.

6 | **American men groom way too much.** The haircut is always perfect. Brad Pitt is an example. He's too polished for me.

7 | **Middle-class guys hide behind big shirts.** Instead, put a T-shirt under your suit. There are so many good clothes out there. Wear chinos with a beautiful long-sleeve T-shirt.

8 | **I watch a lot of TV. Larry King, he's the only anchorman that I love.** He has his own style—he has personality I'm not saying that they should all be like Larry King, but he's much better than Bill O'Reilly.

9 | **When it comes to their bodies, men should be less pumped.** There's too much muscle. American guys should do more swimming. It's a better sport because it tones your body but it doesn't pump you up so that you look unrealistic.

10 | **Men should stop worrying about business so much.** Everything is money, money, money. You should be thinking about seducing women, which men have forgotten how to do.

ACCESSORIES

CHAPTER 13

Good style is about making a statement. Sometimes that means shouting from the rooftops; other times, a higher degree of discretion is called for. Accessories enable you to add personality and flare to your look by using subtle accents. Just remember to keep it simple.

HATS, SCARVES, AND GLOVES

HATS

Blame J.F.K. When Kennedy appeared bare-headed at his inauguration in 1961 a wave of change swept across the country that signaled the demise of the hat. Before the 1960s men wore hats, almost without exception, when they left home. The social and cultural changes that occurred in the sixties and seventies, and the boom in casual dressing and sportswear that followed, have seen hat sales, except perhaps for baseball caps, tank.

You probably don't own many hats—maybe a couple of woolen ones for the winter and ball caps for the summer—but it's fair to say that, if you've got the stomach for it, a well-worn piece of headgear can prove a stylish way to demonstrate your individuality. Like so many other components of menswear, the basic rule of wearing hats is to keep it simple. Avoid anything "novelty" meant to amuse or that has a logo on it that doesn't belong to a sports team. Stick with classics like the fedora in a time-honored silhouette. If you're worried about looking like gramps, take a look around your favorite stores—top designers have updated many shapes and styles for the modern man. Most importantly, always remember to take your hat off when you're talking to a lady.

OPTIONS

LEATHER GLOVES
Simple, elegant, and functional, leather gloves are a must-have in the winter months.

FEDORA
Although the popularity of hats has declined since the fifties, the fedora is a classic that won't disappear.

DRIVING CAP
A distinctively English style that has taken on a hip-hop flavor. The driving cap looks best with rough woolens and cloth coats.

KNIT HAT
Keep warm with a snug knit hat. Choose one that doesn't droop over your eyebrows or form a peak on top of your head.

BASEBALL CAP
Not just for the park anymore, baseball caps come in more upscale fabrics and colors.

COTTON SCARF
When it's cool rather than chilly, a cotton scarf in a bright color offers flare when matched with a dark suit.

COLLEGE SCARF
A traditional, colorful way to show your allegiance to your alma mater—and keep yourself warm too.

WINTER SCARF
Choose your winter scarf with care—a chunky version will overwhelm your suit and coat. Go for a thinner version in cashmere.

BELTS

BELTS

Belts are essential to a man's wardrobe, not only because they keep your pants up but also because they help to pull an outfit together. Your everyday go-to belt should be simple and in black calfskin. Beyond that you can move on to brown leather and even to experimenting with the materials your belts are made from. If you can afford it, crocodile is a stylish option. Console yourself with the thought that, treated right, a crocodile belt could last a lifetime.

Unless you work at a rodeo, you should make sure that the buckle is simple and elegant. No words or logos, please. A classic black or brown belt can last years, so don't be afraid to push the boat out. Think of it as an investment.

Once you've mastered the basics you can add a thick belt to your collection. These are great for pairing with dressier outfits as long as they are discrete. Wear them in a clashing color and you'll look like a member of a new-wave band from the eighties. Wide belts are more casual and can be paired with jeans for a western look. The most casual belts are in suede, cloth, canvas, or nylon. Keep these for informal occasions only.

HOW TO MATCH YOUR BELT

Your belt should match your shoes: black shoes, black belt; brown shoes, brown belt. More casual belts offer a few more options, and allow you to play with brighter colors and patterns.

OPTIONS

BLACK
A slim black-leather belt with simple hardware is versatile enough to wear with any pants in your closet.

BROWN
Brown belts and shoes go better with lighter colors and are a great bridge between light pants and colored shirts.

WOVEN LEATHER
A braided belt is a summer favorite that should be worn with slim-cut pants and collared shirts.

SKINNY
Keep a skinny belt on hand for those high-waisted pants.

CLOTH
Cloth belts are a casual choice that works well with well-worn khakis or jeans. Pair with T-shirts and polos in solid colors.

GLASSES AND SUNGLASSES

HOW TO FIT

We've all been there. You walk into a store and impulsively purchase a pair of glasses or sunglasses. You wear them once and decide that they make you look like Bingo from the Banana Splits. So you throw them in a drawer and leave them there with the other half dozen pairs you own that have barely seen the light of day. The moral of the story—don't go freestyle when buying glasses. Before you make a purchase have a long, hard think about the shape of your face and what types of frames would best suit you.

Ask your optician to fit your frames properly and get the lightest weight lenses possible so that you're not constantly pushing them up the bridge of your nose. If your prescription necessitates heavy lenses, get a pair of frames with ear loops, or be sure that the temples fit snugly enough to keep your glasses securely on your head.

(A) TRIANGULAR FACE

If you have a broad forehead and a narrow chin, choose glasses that mimic your bone structure and help to accentuate the eyes. A pair of aviators would work well. And consider the lenses: bold tints won't don't work with glasses like this, so consider gradient lenses.

B OVAL FACE

Long, lean faces need frames that accentuate width. Forget delicate, John Lennon-style glasses and opt for heavy plastic wraparound and frames with oversize lenses.

C ROUND FACE

Full cheeks and a curved jaw line call for frames with a contrasting, angular shape. In order to create a sense of balance, make sure the corners are slightly rounded, not sharp.

JEWELRY

WATCHES

Whether you're trying to demonstrate to the world that you're a sophisticate, an adventurer or that you just got a bonus equal to the GDP of a small African republic, there's no easier way than through your watch. One word of advice: unless you're a Cash Money Millionaire, go easy on the bling.

DAYTIME

For daytime and weekends, get a metal-bracelet diving or pilot's watch. You might not need all the functions while on your morning commute, but they make a powerful masculine statement.

....

NIGHTTIME

For nights out or if you work in an upscale environment, invest in a plain-faced watch with a leather strap. Sometimes making a statement involves less rather than more.

CUFF LINKS

Cuff links are a safe way for men to express their individuality and appeal to those who want to stand out from the chino-wearing crowd. They offer an edge of formality to an outfit, so they are not really suited for casual wear. However, in the right environment—work, a smart dinner, a formal event—they offer a high degree of sophistication. Just be sure to keep it classy: while it might sound a little excessive, it's worth splashing out for a pair in platinum or gold.

! In 1989, Patek Philippe created **the most involved timepiece to date**, a pocket watch called the Caliber 89. **It has 1,728 parts, and its displays include a map of 2,800 stars.**

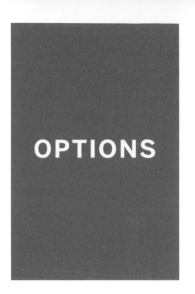

OPTIONS

LEATHER BAND

At a low-key dinner party leave the year-end-bonus watch at home and go with a less in-your-face time-piece. A band in black crocodile and a simple white or silver face will offer an impression of classic sophistication.

STAINLESS STEEL STRAP

The most adaptable and stylish everyday watch a man can own. Sporty dial markings temper the dressiness of the shiny steel brace-let, making the timepiece elegant, not flashy. Think Paul Newman, rather than Donald Trump.

T-BACK

Classic T-back cuff links should be the foundation of a man's collec-tion. A pair in silver or gold goes with formal spread-collar shirts as well as with more casual styles.

ROUND

As versatile as T-backs, solid round silver or gold cuff links—err on the small side—can be dressed up or down.

DIGITAL

The Casio watch of the eighties endures as a classic. Just wear it and other chunky black digital watches with appropriate attire—e.g. jeans and casual button-down shirts, not suits.

SPORT WATCHES

A sporty watch is an essential—you can't wear a dressy platinum time-piece with a polo shirt and beat-up jeans. Invest in a chronograph with a matte metal dial and a rubber or canvas band.

ENAMEL WATCH

A chronograph watch with an enamel dial is just slightly less for-mal than one rimmed with steel. Which sporty watch you choose is a matter of preference but the rules are the same: Wear it with casual clothes, not suits.

KNOT

The knot is a timeless cuff-link style that suits French-cuff shirts worn in a less formal way—with a navy blazer instead of a black-tie outfit, for example.

GEOMETRIC

Experiment with cuff links in as many shapes as you like—from artsy circular shapes to simple rect-angles. Just steer clear of anything oversize or diamond-encrusted.

HOW TO PULL OFF

Jewelry

There's a school of thought that the only pieces of jewelry a man should own are a wedding ring and a watch. While a blanket "no jewelry" maxim is worth sticking to when it comes to skull rings and World Series of Poker bracelets, it doesn't work for everyone.

If you want to wear jewelry there's one rule that you absolutely have to stick to: keep it really simple. If you want to make a statement, make a statement—but don't make two or three. Stick to a single item like an ID bracelet or diamond stud. A word of warning: if you're going to go over the top, be prepared to live with the consequences, Mr. T.

● ○ ○

● ● ○

● ● ●

BEGINNER
Learn to wear a watch well. You don't have to spend a lot of money to have a range of watches for different occasions. Once you've mastered getting the right watch to go with the appropriate clothes, you're ready to move up.

INTERMEDIATE
Start with a classic signet ring or simple ID bracelet. Jewelry with meaningful ties to family, schools, teams, or accomplishments is always better than mere ornaments.

ADVANCED
60 Minutes correspondent Ed Bradley wore a gold hoop in his ear; Johnny Depp wears necklaces. The secret to wearing jewelry well is having confidence and sticking with a signature look.

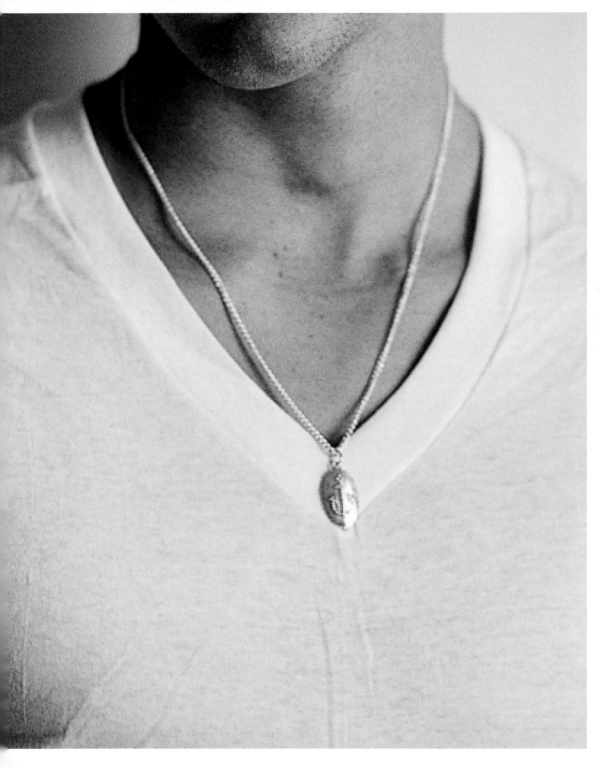

BAGS AND WALLETS

BAGS

Men are scared of bags. We think of them as feminine, preferring instead to cram our pockets full and carry precarious piles of stuff. Given that most of us now carry around a cell phone, BlackBerry, iPod, gym clothes, and reading material, it's time to get over bag phobia in favor of a stylish and practical solution.

Find a bag that's appropriate to your clothes: For instance, guys in suits shouldn't carry shoulder bags, which can bunch up the shoulders of your jacket.

The briefcase is the old stand-by. From hard, hinged, and structured to soft and fluid, it's a reliable option.

For casual days, backpacks and messenger bags still are practical choices; just make sure that you choose one that won't make you look like you're still in college.

For weekends away and vacations, most top designers make elegant leather duffels and carryalls for men. Practical and luxurious, they'll have you looking first class even if you're traveling coach.

OPTIONS

LEATHER CARRYALL

If you can spring for a luxurious version of the classic carryall it will serve you well.

WORK BAG

You'll be taken more seriously at work with a sturdy, practical briefcase.

WEEKEND BAG

Shrug off the stress of the working week with an elegant structured travel bag that's got the pliability of a duffel.

CANVAS CARRYALL

Sturdy canvas bags with elegant leather trim defy categorization. Use one to carry a laptop, a squash racquet, or a weekend's worth of clothes.

BACKPACK
The classic backpack doesn't have to be geeky if it's made of canvas or sleek leather.

MESSENGER
You've got so much stuff to carry these days you might as well get a bag that fits easily over your shoulder to ease the burden.

ROLLING BAG
Wheelie bags are indispensable for frequent fliers.

DOPP KIT
Every man should own a smartly curated Dopp kit for weekends away and trips abroad.

ZIP-CLOSURE WALLET
Wallets should be simple. A zip-up case keeps everything in place.

BILLFOLD WALLET
An elegant black wallet that fits easily inside your jacket pocket is one of the most basic items a man should own.

TRAVEL WALLET
A travel wallet will save you from rooting around in your bag when you've got tickets and passports to carry.

Pack

Care

Shop

How to Pack

HOW TO PACK

WHETHER YOU'RE HEADING OFF FOR TWO WEEKS IN BALI OR THREE DAYS IN LONDON, PACKING IS A CHORE. TO MAKE IT QUICK AND SIMPLE FOLLOW THESE BASIC STEPS.

1. Edit your wardrobe and only prepare essentials ready to be packed. For a trip of three days or less, think about wearing a suit and taking enough shirts, sweaters, and ties to last you four or five changes.

2. Set your bag on a bed or sofa. Place with the heaviest items at the bottom of the suitcase: shoes, sneakers, dopp kit, and gadgets. Roll up T-shirts and underwear and place them along the sides of the case.

3. Stuff your shoes with socks and place a rolled-up tie in the heel. Note: Slip your wing tips into drawstring shoe bags before you pack them. This will protect the shoe's leather and shine—and keep your clothes from getting dirtied too.

4. If you're skipping the garment bag, turn your suit jacket inside out and fold it into quarters (with the first fold being across the center of the back). This should prevent the worst of the wrinkles. When you arrive at your destination, hang the jacket in the bathroom and take a hot shower. The steam should remove any creases.

5. Lay your shirts flat on top of everything else in the bag and have them pressed, if necessary, once you arrive.

6. Some people place layers of tissue paper between their clothes. That's unnecessary. The key to keeping your clothes rumple-free is not over-stuffing your bag.

Business Trip

- [ ] 2 suits
- [ ] 5 shirts
- [ ] 1 turtleneck
- [ ] 1 pair of jeans or chinos
- [ ] 4 ties
- [ ] 4 pocket squares
- [ ] 5 pairs socks
- [ ] 5 pairs of underwear

Long Weekend

- [ ] 1 blazer
- [ ] 1 striped shirt
- [ ] 2 casual shirts—polo or T-shirt and camp shirt
- [ ] 1 pair of chinos
- [ ] 1 pair of jeans
- [ ] Boots or walking shoes
- [ ] 3 pairs of socks—at least one pair of athletic socks
- [ ] 2 pairs of underwear
- [ ] 1 belt

Vacation

- [ ] 2 pairs of jeans—blue, gray, black, or white
- [ ] 1 pair of shorts
- [ ] 1 pair of chinos
- [ ] 1 pair dress pants
- [ ] 2 polos
- [ ] 2 shirts
- [ ] 1 pair of boots or walking shoes

- [ ] 1 pair of loafers
- [ ] 1 blazer
- [ ] 1 sweater
- [ ] Socks and underwear for 7 days
- [ ] 1 pair of athletic socks
- [ ] Workout clothes
- [ ] 1 swimsuit

How to Care

HOW TO CARE FOR YOUR WARDROBE

There's no point in spending money on clothes if you're not going to take care of them. Natural fibers like wool, cotton, and leather need to breathe to stay fresh and wear well, so don't cram your clothes into closets or stuff them in drawers. Give them room. As far as suits and coats go, make use of the storage bags you received when you made your purchase. The same goes for shoes—protect them by storing them in their boxes.

SHOES
Shoes should be shined often and not just so they look good. The polish moisturizes and seals the leather, protecting it from moisture. You cap-toe shoes will stand up to the grind of daily life better if they have a good coating of polish. Have shoes repaired before they get too worn-down. New heels and soles will keep your shoes in top condition. Plus, the uppers will wear better and last longer.

Washing Instructions

Drying Instructions

Dry cleaning Instructions

Ironing Instructions

Things You Should Hang

SUITS

Invest in good-quality wooden hangers for your suits. Use the type with a simple wooden bar across the middle. And never hang your suit pants with pinching clips or bars.

PANTS

Gently drape your pants over the hanger about a third of the way up the leg. That will keep the crease sharp.

TIES

Tie racks are a time-tested essential. Use one.

SHIRTS

To hang shirts or to fold them is one of the great debate of the sartorial world. The fact is, it makes very little difference. Do what works for you and your space. But there's little difference between hanging your shirts on a hanger and keeping them folded in a drawer.

Things You Should Fold

UNDERWEAR

Undershirts, socks, and pajamas all belong in drawers. Whether you separate them is up to you.

POCKET SQUARES

Even if your repertoire doesn't extend beyond white, every guy needs a few, crisply ironed pocket squares. Store them in a dresser drawer, away from riff-raff like running shorts.

T-SHIRTS AND POLOS

They'll keep their shape better in a drawer than on the hanger. Just fold them neatly.

SWEATERS

Like water, gravity is the enemy of wool. Preserve the shape of your sweaters by folding them and placing in a drawer or on a shelf.

Laundry Basics

Let's start with the basics: Most of what you need to know about your clothes is printed on a little tag inside the garment. If it says dry clean only—then dry clean it. Otherwise, you should wash and dry the garment as suggested. If you wear a suit or at least a blazer and a tie several times a week, there isn't much in your closet that needs to be washed. Your underclothes and socks go in with the whites or the colors, wash in warm or hot water. Your casual shirts, jeans, and khakis can take whichever cycle you like best: Cold will preserve the color and hot will increase the softness and fade. Pretreat stains before you toss the laundry in.

Your dress shirts should be washed, never dry cleaned. If you don't want to wash them yourself, remember that the machinery most cleaners use to wash and press your shirts can be very unforgiving. You can ask for "no machine press" when you drop your shirts off to be laundered.

After you've mastered the washing machine don't forget the dryer. It's surprising how many men remain confused by these machines. They're there; they're convenient; why not use them correctly? Remember that excessive heat is a no-no for your clothes: They'll shrink and they'll fade. Using the permanent press setting will reduce wrinkling. And take the clothes out right after the cycle is finished. Even better, consider allowing your shirts to air dry on a hanger and your sweaters to dry flat on a towel.

Finally, get an iron and learn how to use it. Being able to touch up a shirt and knowing how to remove wrinkles from your pants will give you an advantage in the real world.

Dry-Cleaning Basics

It's pretty simple. Dry clean your clothes as little as possible. Natural fibers don't require as much cleaning as you would think. Obviously, things like cashmere and other knits need to be dry cleaned after several wearings, but err on the side of caution unless the garment is stained. Even then, see if your dry cleaner can spot clean the area. And, if you wear an undershirt as well as a shirt, your body isn't coming into much contact with your clothes.

Caring for a Wool Suit

A good wool suit is much less high-maintenance than you think. In fact, dry cleaning is not great for it. It puts unnecessary stress on the garment that will cause it to wear out much sooner than it should.

Get yourself a good long-handled clothes brush with stiff bristles. The brush will remove most of the dirt and stains (after they've dried) that you can expect. At night, when you take your suit off, brush the jacket once from the shoulders to the vents and down along the chest. Don't forget to brush the pants—especially the front of the legs.

You should also brush a suit once you've put it on in the morning. This vigorous brushing will keep the suit free of anything that will make it dirty over the long run. Steam the suit to eliminate any wrinkles.

Once or twice a year, have your suit dry cleaned and properly pressed. When you store it, be sure that it is on a good hanger with wide shoulders or tissue paper. Extended periods of time on a wire hanger will make the suit lose its shape. And never store it inside the dry cleaner's plastic wrap. Wool needs to breathe to stay vital.

Where to Shop

WHERE TO SHOP
Where to Buy What's Inside: Selected Retailers

ARIZONA

The Clothierie
2552 E. Camelback Rd.
Phoenix, AZ 85016
(602) 956-8600

CALIFORNIA

A B Fits
1519 Grant Ave.
San Francisco, CA 94133
(415) 982-5726

Agnes B.
100 N. Robertson Blvd.
Los Angeles, CA 90048
(310) 271-9643

Alpha Male
8625 Melrose Ave.
West Hollywood, CA 90069
(310) 855-0775

American Rag
150 S. La Brea Ave.
Los Angeles, CA 90036
(323) 935-3157

Barneys New York
9570 Wilshire Blvd.
Beverly Hills, CA 90212
(310) 276-4400

Blue Bee
913 State St.
Santa Barbara, CA 93101
(805) 882-2468

Bobby Jones
310 North Beverly Dr.
Beverly Hills, CA 90210
(310) 860-9566

Bryan Lee
1840 Union St.
San Francisco, CA 94123
(415) 923-9923

Built By Wendy
7938 W. Third St.
Los Angeles, CA 90048
(323) 651-1902

Christian Dior
8500 Beverly Blvd.
Los Angeles, CA 90048
(310) 659-5875

Costume National
8920 Melrose Ave.
West Hollywood, CA 90069
(310) 273-0100

Douglas Fir
8311 W. Third St.
Los Angeles, CA 90048
(323) 651-5445

Energie
8070 Melrose Ave.
Los Angeles, CA 90046
(323) 655-7220

Fred Segal
8118 Melrose Ave.
Los Angeles, CA 90046
(323) 651-1935

Gianni Versace
248 N. Rodeo Dr.
Beverly Hills, CA 90210
(310) 205-3921

Gimmie Shoes
416 Hayes St.
San Francisco, CA 94102
(415) 864-0691

Jack's
2260 Chestnut St.
San Francisco, CA 94123
(415) 567-3673

James Perse
8914 Melrose Ave.
Los Angeles, CA 90069
(310) 276-7277

Just Cavalli
8647 W. Sunset Blvd.
West Hollywood, CA 90069
(310) 492-0101

Kitson For Men
146 N. Robertson Blvd.
Los Angeles, CA 90048
(310) 358-9550

Riley James
3027 Fillmore St.
San Francisco, CA 94123
(415) 775-7956

Rolo
2351 Market St.
San Francisco, CA 94114
(415) 431-4545

Ron Herman
8100 Melrose Ave.
Los Angeles, CA 90046
(323) 651-4129

Scout LA
7920 W. Third St.
West Hollywood, CA 90048
(323) 658-8684

Stussy LA
112 S. La Brea Ave.
Los Angeles, CA 90048
(323) 933-2251

Weathervane
1132 Montana Ave.
Santa Monica, CA 90403
(310) 395-0397

Wilkes Bashford
375 Sutter St.
San Francisco, CA 94108
(415) 986-4380

COLORADO

**John Lobb at
Lawrence Covell**
252 Steele St.
Denver, CO 80206
(303) 320-1023

Skye Clothing
1499 Blake St., #1A
Denver, CO 80202
(303) 623-0444

Urban Outfitters
934 Pearl St.
Boulder, CO 80302
(303) 706-0226

CONNECTICUT

Darien Sport Shop
1127 Post Rd.
Darien, CT 06820
(203) 655-2575

J. Press
262 York St.
New Haven, CT 06511
(203) 787-0377

Mitchells
670 Post Rd. East
Westport, CT 06880
(203) 227-5165

Richards
359 Greenwich Ave.
Greenwich, CT 06830
(203) 622-0551

DISTRICT OF COLUMBIA

GT Players
1328 Wisconsin Ave. NW
Washington, D.C. 20007
(202) 333-7426

Ralph Lauren
1245 Wisconsin Ave. NW
Washington, DC 20007
(202) 965-0905

Sherman Pickey
1647 Wisconsin Ave. NW
Washington, DC 20007
(202) 333-4212

Sterling & Burke Ltd.
1025 Connecticut Ave. NW
Suite 1012
Washington, DC 20036
(202) 331-4244

FLORIDA

Etro
342 San Lorenzo Ave.
Coral Gables, FL 33146
(305) 569-0793

Leo
640 Collins Ave.
Miami, FL 33160
(305) 531-6550

Napapijri
1008 Lincoln Rd.
Miami Beach, FL 33139
(305) 695-7301

Original Penguin
925 Lincoln Rd.
Miami, FL 33139
(305) 673-0722

Scoop Shore Club
1901 Collins Ave.
Miami Beach, FL 33139
(305) 532-5929

Tomas Maier Pool Wear
1800 W. Ave.
Miami Beach, FL 33139
(305) 531-8383

Trillion Men's & Women's
315 Worth Ave.
Palm Beach, FL 33480
(561) 832-3525

GEORGIA

Bill Hallman
792 N. Highland Ave. NE
Atlanta, GA 30306
(404) 876-6055

Blue Genes
3400 Around Lenox Dr. NE
Suite 294
Atlanta, GA 30326
(404) 231-3400

Bobby Jones Sportswear
3393 Peachtree Rd. NE
Atlanta, GA 30326
(404) 846-7977

DressCodes
201 W. Ponce de Leon Ave.
Decatur, GA 30030
(404) 343-2894

Fab'rik
1114 W. Peachtree St.
Atlanta, GA 30309
(404) 881-8223

Marc by Marc Jacobs
322 West Broughton St.
Savannah GA 34101
(912) 234-2800

ILLINOIS

Active Endeavors
853 W. Armitage Ave.
Chicago, IL 60614
(773) 281-8100

Apartment Number Nine
1804 North Damen Ave.
Chicago, IL 60647
(773) 395-2999

Guise
2217 N. Halstead St.
Chicago, IL 60614
(773) 929-6101

Hejfina
1529 N. Milwaukee Ave.
Chicago, IL 60622
(773) 772-0002

Jake
3740 N. Southport Ave.
Chicago, IL 60613
(773) 929-5253

Jil Sander
48 East Oak St.
Chicago, IL 60611
(312) 335-0006

Mark Shale
900 N. Michigan Ave.
Chicago, IL 60611
(312) 440-0720

Untitled
2705 N. Clark St.
Chicago, IL 60614
(773) 404-9225

LOUISIANA

Saks Fifth Avenue
301 Canal St.
New Orleans, LA 70130
(504) 524-2200

MARYLAND

South Moon Under
815 Aliceanna St.
Baltimore, MD 21202
(410) 685-7820

Yves Saint Laurent
5516 Wisconsin Ave.
Chevy Chase, MD 20815
(301) 652-2250

MASSACHUSETTS

The Andover Shop
234 Clarendon St.
Boston, MA 02116
(617) 266-6100

Louis Boston
234 Berkley St.
Boston, MA 02116
(617) 262-6100

Maxwell & Co.
200 Main St.
Falmouth, MA 02540
(508) 540-8752

Murray's Toggery Shop
62 Main St.
Nantucket, MA 02554
(508) 228-0437

Riccardi
116 Newbury St.
Boston, MA 02116
(617) 266-3158

MICHIGAN

Bivouac
334 S. State St.
Ann Arbor, MI 48104
(877) 846-8248

Caruso Caruso
166 W. Maple Rd.
Birmingham, MI 48009
(248) 645-5151

Peasant
205 E. Maple Rd.
Birmingham, MI 48009
(248) 203-6470

Macy's
700 Briarwood Circle
Ann Arbor, MI 48108
(734) 998-5000

Nordstrom's
2850 W. Big Beaver Rd.
Troy, MI 48084
(248) 816-5100

MINNESOTA

Len Druskin
3140 Galleria Edina
Minneapolis, MN 55435
(952) 927-7923

MISSOURI

Level 1 Menswear
314 N. Euclid Ave.
Saint Louis, MO 63108
(314) 361-7565

NEBRASKA

Allen Edmonds
10303 Pacific St.
Omaha, NE 68113
(402) 392-1967

Ralph Lauren
17255 Davenport St.
Omaha, NE 68118
(402) 289-2942

NEVADA

Christian Dior
3600 Las Vegas Blvd.
Las Vegas, NV 89109
(800) 929-3467

Marc Jacobs, Las Vegas
3500 Las Vegas Blvd.
Las Vegas, NV 89109
(702) 369-2007

NEW YORK

Alfred Dunhill
711 Fifth Ave.
New York, NY 10022
(212) 753-9292

An Earnest Cut & Sew
821 Washington St.
New York, NY 10014
(212) 242-3414

T. Anthony
445 Park Ave.
New York, NY 10022
(212) 750-9797

A.P.C.
131 Mercer St.
New York, NY 10012
(212) 966-9685

Atrium
644 Broadway
New York, NY 10012
(212) 473-9200

Audemars Piguet
40 E. 57th St.
New York, NY 10022
(212) 688-6644

Balenciaga
542 W. 22nd St.
New York, NY 10011
(212) 206-0872

Barker Black Ltd
198 Elizabeth St.
New York, NY 10012
(212) 966-2166

Bergdorf Goodman
754 Fifth Ave.
New York, NY 10019
(212) 753-7300

Berluti
971 Madison Ave.
New York, NY 10021
(212) 439-6400

Big Drop Men
1325 Third Ave.
New York, NY 10021
(212) 472-3200

Bloomingdale's Soho
504 Broadway
New York, NY 10012
(212) 729-5900

Brioni
57 E. 57th St.
New York, NY 10022
(212) 376-5777

Camouflage
139 Eighth Ave.
New York, NY 10011
(212) 741-5173

Cellini
509 Madison Ave.
New York, NY 10022
(212) 888-0505

Charles Tyrwhitt
745 Seventh Ave.
New York, NY 10019
(212) 764-4697

Church's English Shoes
689 Madison Ave.
New York, NY 10021
(212) 758-5200

Classic Kicks
298 Elizabeth St.
New York, NY 10012
(212) 979-9514

Comme des Garçons
520 W. 22nd St.
New York, NY 10011
(212) 604-9200

DisRespectacles
82 Christopher St.
New York, NY 10014
(212) 741-9550

Diesel Denim Gallery
68 Greene St.
New York, NY 10012
(212) 966-5593

Duncan Quinn
8 Spring St.
New York, NY 10012
(212) 226-7030

Flying A
169 Spring St.
New York, NY 10012
(212) 965-9090

Gant
645 Fifth Ave.
New York, NY 10022
(212) 813-9170

Ghurka
683 Madison Ave.
New York, NY 10021
(212) 826-8300

Gianfranco Ferré
85 Fifth Ave.
New York, NY 10003
(212) 414-5759

J. Lindeberg, New York
126 Spring St.
New York, NY 10012
(212) 625-9403

Jack Spade
56 Greene St.
New York, NY 10012
(212) 625-1820

Jeffrey New York
449 W. 14th St.
New York, NY 10014
(212) 255-2434

Lounge
593 Broadway
New York, NY 10012
(212) 226-7585

L'Uomo
383 Bleecker St.
New York, NY 10014
(212) 206-1844

Maison Martin Margiela
803 Greenwich St.
New York, NY 10014
(212) 989-7612

Malo
814 Madison Ave.
New York, NY 10021
(212) 396-4721

Nom de Guerre
640 Broadway
New York, NY 10012
(212) 253-2707

Paul Smith
108 Fifth Ave.
New York, NY 10011
(212) 627-9770

Porsche Design
624 Madison Ave.
New York, NY 10022
(212) 308-1786

Oak
668 President St.
Brooklyn, NY 11215
(718) 857-2080

Odin
328 E. 11th St.
New York, NY 10003
(212) 475-0666

Opening Ceremony
35 Howard St.
New York, NY 10013
(212) 219-2688

Robert Talbott
680 Madison Ave.
New York, NY 10021
(212) 751-1200

Rogan Store
91 Franklin St.
New York, NY 10013
(646) 827-7554

Saks Fifth Avenue
611 Fifth Ave.
New York, NY 10022
(212) 753-4000

Salvatore Ferragamo
661 Fifth Ave.
New York, NY 10022
(212) 759-3822

Scoop
473 Broadway
New York, NY 10012
(212) 925-3539

Steven Alan, New York
229 Elizabeth St.
New York, NY 10012
(212) 226-7482

Thom Browne New York
100 Hudson St.
New York, NY 10013
(212) 633-1197

Thomas Pink
520 Madison Ave
New York, NY 10022
(212) 838-1928

Tiecoon Inc.
400 Seventh Ave.
New York, NY 10001
(212) 904-1433

Tod's
650 Madison Ave.
New York, NY 10022
(212) 644-5945

Tous
109 Greene St.
New York, NY 10012
(212) 219-1444

Turnbull & Asser
42 E. 57th St.
New York, NY 10022
(212) 752-5700

Uniqlo
155 Spring St.
New York, NY 10012
(212) 334-4193

UNIS
226 Elizabeth St.
New York, NY 10012
(212) 431-5533

Valentino
747 Madison Ave.
New York, NY 10021
(212) 772-6969

What Comes Around Goes Around
351 W. Broadway
New York, NY 10013
(212) 343-9303

Yohji Yamamoto
103 Grand St.
New York, NY 10013
(212) 966-9066

NORTH CAROLINA

Neiman Marcus
4400 Sharon Rd.
Charlotte, NC 28211
(704) 442-7900

Old Dog Clothing
1515 E. Fourth St.
Charlotte, NC 28204
(704) 347-4712

OHIO

Cole Haan
1500 Polaris Pkwy.
Columbus, OH 43240
(614) 781-1250

Denim
3212 Madison Rd.
Cincinnati, OH 45209
(513) 321-1892

Karisma
32 E. High St.
Oxford, OH 45056
(513) 523-9300

OREGON

Mario's
806 SW Broadway
Portland, OR 97205
(503) 241-5034

PENNSYLVANIA

Bloomingdale's
The Court at King of Prussia
2 Rt. 202 North
660 West DeKalb Pike
King of Prussia, PA 19406
(610) 337-6300

Charlie's Jeans
210 Market St.
Philadelphia, PA 19106
(215) 923-9681

The London Shop
339 Northhampton St.
Easton, PA 18180
(610) 258-0161

Sailor Jerry
304 Walnut Street
Philadelphia, PA 19106
(215) 923 6980

South Moon Under
1731 Chestnut St.
Philadelphia, PA 19103
(215) 563-2298

Ubiq
1509 Walnut St.
Philadelphia, PA 19107
(215) 988-0194

RHODE ISLAND

American Apparel
159 Weybosset St.
Providence, RI 02903
(401) 861-0007

SOUTH CAROLINA

Ben Silver
149 King St.
Charleston, SC 29401
(843) 577-4556

TEXAS

Barneys New York
8687 North Central
Expressway
Dallas, TX 75225
(469) 221-4700

Factory People
1325 S. Congress St.
Austin, TX 78704
(512) 440-8002

Forty Five Ten
4510 McKinney Ave.
Dallas, TX 75205
(214) 559-4510

Neiman Marcus
1618 Main St.
Dallas, TX 75201
(214) 741-6911

Stanley Korshak Men's
500 Crescent Ct.
Dallas, TX 75201
(214) 871-3610

VIRGINIA

Eljo's Inc.
1067 Millmont St.
Charlottesville, VA 22903
(434) 295-5230

Dillard's
9208 Stony Point Pkwy.
Richmond, VA 23235
(804) 253-1860

WASHINGTON

Barneys New York
City Centre 1420 5th Ave.
Suite 110
Seattle, WA 98101
(206) 622-6300

David Lawrence
1318 Fourth Avenue
Seattle, WA 98101
(206) 622-2544

Mario's
1513 Sixth Ave.
Seattle, WA 98101
(206) 223-1461

CANADA

French Connection
1182 Sainte Catherines St.
West
Montreal, Quebec H3B 1K1
(514) 908 -1506

Harry Rosen
Pacific Centre
700 West Georgia St.
Vancouver, BC V7Y1EB
(604) 683-6861

Michel Brisson
1012 Laurier West
Montreal, Quebec H2V 2K8
(514) 270-1012

Mont Blanc
151 Bloor Street West
Toronto, Ontario M5S 1S4
(416) 925-4810¥

Ray Rickburn
2100 West 4th Avenue
Vancouver, BC V6K1N6
(604) 738-9177

ACKNOWLEDGMENTS

This book would not have been possible without the efforts of several members of *Details'* staff:

Greg Williams, Deputy Editor; Katherine Wheelock, Features Editor; Matthew Edelstein, Fashion Editor; the *Details* fashion department: Micah Johnson, Matthew Marden, and Eugene Tong; Rockwell Harwood, Creative Director; Andrea Oliveri, Special Projects Editor; Diana Benbasset, Managing Editor; and Chris Mitchell, Vice President and Publisher and his advertising and promotion staff.

Finally, I'd like to thank my wife, Sarah, for her extraordinary patience during the completion of this book. No woman should ever have to watch her husband run to the office at midnight to write about how a man's ass should look in his jeans.

This book was produced by:
Melcher Media, Inc.
124 West 13th Street
New York, NY 10011
www.melcher.com

Publisher: Charles Melcher
Associate Publisher: Bonnie Eldon
Editor in Chief: Duncan Bock
Project Editor: Betty Wong
Assistant Editor: Lindsey Stanberry
Editorial Assistant: Daniel del Valle
Production Director: Kurt Andrews

Design: Volume Inc.

Melcher Media wishes to thank:
Anna Bernabe, Graeme Boyle, Bettina Budewig, David E. Brown, Lisa Dorffi, Laura Gardner, Eric Heiman, Marion Maneker, Lauren Marino, Charles Masters, Jens Mortensen, Andrea Nakayama, Lauren Nathan, John Olson, Alessandra Rafferty, Lia Ronnen, Holly Rothman, Solange Sandstrom, Bill Shinker, Ellen Sitkin, Shoshana Thaler, Marcelo Viana, Kim Bello Weiss, and Megan Worman.

CREDITS

Clothing and Accessory Credits

CHAPTER 1: SHIRTS

Pages 14–15: Shirts Polo by Ralph Lauren, Emporio Armani, Banana Republic, Izod, Etro, Steven Alan, Lorenzini, Pierre Cardin, Burberry London, Dolce & Gabbana. **Page 18:** Shirt by Turnbull & Asser. **Pages 20–21:** Top row, from left: Shirts by Brooks Brothers, Dunhill, Etro, Brioni, Hickey. Bottom row, from left: Shirts by Thom Browne, Ralph Lauren, Marc Jacobs, Comme des Garçons, Hermès, Bamford and Sons. **Page 22:** Shirt by Michael Bastian. **Page 24:** Top row, from left: Shirts by Brooks Brothers, Charles Tyrwhitt, Brooks Brothers. Bottom row, from left: Shirts by Brooks Brothers. **Pages 26–27:** From left: Shirt by Prada. Suit by Dior Homme. Tie by Band of Outsiders. Tie bar by Tiffany's. Shoes by Dries Van Noten. Jeans by Levi's. Belt by Dsquared². Shoes by Cole Haan. Shirt by Prada. Coat by Burberry. Blazer by Prada. Trousers by Michael Kors. Scarf by Ralph Lauren. Gloves by Coach. Boots by Brooks Brothers (Peel & Co.). Sweater by Martin Margiela. Sneakers by Common Projects. **Page 29:** Shirt by Hickey.

CHAPTER 2: PANTS

Pages 34–35: Pants by Gucci. **Page 38:** Pants by Isaia. **Pages 40–41:** From left: Pants by DKNY, DKNY, J. Crew, Giorgio Armani, Ralph Lauren. **Pages 42–43:** From left: Pants by Paul Smith, Polo by Ralph Lauren, Polo by Ralph Lauren, Rogan, Zegna. **Pages 48–49:** Top row, from left: Shorts by Rogan, Polo by Ralph Lauren, Kenneth Cole. Bottom row, from left: Shorts by Adidas, Tommy Hilfiger, Diesel. **Pages 50–51:** From left: Pants by Marc Jacobs. Blazer by Narciso Rodriguez. Shirt by Jil Sander. Tie by Steven Alan. Tie bar by Bulgari. Shoes by Cole Haan. Shirt by J. Crew. Sweater by Banana Republic. Belt by Hugo Boss. Shoes by Prada. Pants by Marc Jacobs. Overcoat by TSE. Shirt by Marc by Marc Jacobs. Tie by Acne Jeans. Denim jacket by Earnest Sewn. Pullover by Tim Hamilton. Polo by Hickey. Shoes by Clarks. **Page 53:** Clockwise from left: Jeans by Diesel, John Varvatos Star USA, AG Adriano Goldschmied, DKNY, Levi's, Z Zegna, Gucci, Sixty.

CHAPTER 3: BLAZERS

Page 58: Blazer by Gucci. Sweater by Timothy Hamilton. Shirt by Tommy Hilfiger. **Page 62:** Blazer by Prada. **Pages 64–65:** Top row, from left: Blazers by Façonnable, Dries Van Noten, Zegna. Bottom row, from left: Blazers by Polo Jeans Co., Burberry, DKNY Jeans, Calvin Klein Collection. **Pages 68–69:** From left: Blazer by Paul Smith. Shirt by Martin Margiela. Chinos by J. Crew. Tie by Steven Alan. Pocket square by Robert Talbott. Belt by Banana Republic. Shoes by Church's. Coat by Nom de Guerre. Shirt by Gucci. Belt by John Varvatos. Shoes by Allen Edmonds. Pants by Michael Kors. Shirt by Dries Van Noten. Jeans by Spurr. Belt by Martin Margiela. Shoes by Ermenegildo Zegna. **Page 71:** Blazer by Tommy Hilfiger. Jeans by A.P.C. Shoes by Converse.

CHAPTER 4: TIES

Pages 76–77: From top to bottom: Ties by Etro, Mulberry, Band of Outsiders, Steven Alan, Polo by Ralph Lauren, Nautica, Thomas Pink. **Pages 78–79:** Top row, from left: Ties by Prada, Prada, Dunhill, A.P.C. Bottom row, from left: Ties by Hermès, J. Press, Dsquared², Ralph Lauren Purple Label. **Page 80:** Shirt and pants by Etro. Tie by J. Press. Tie bar by Bulgari. Belt by Prada. **Pages 86–87:** From left: Shirt by J. Crew. Tie by Kenneth Cole Reaction. Shirt by Ralph Lauren Purple Label. Tie by Kiton. Shirt by Thomas Pick. Tie by Dsquared².

CHAPTER 5: SUITS

Pages 92–93: From left: Suit by Moschino. Shirt by Ennio Capasa for Costume National Homme. Tie by John Varvatos. Suit by Dunhill. Shirt by Van Heusen. Tie by Ralph Lauren Black Label. **Page 96:** Suit by Charles Nolan. **Pages 98–99:** From left: Suits by Ralph Lauren, Tommy Hilfiger, Brooks Brothers. **Pages 100–101:** From left: Suits by Marc Jacobs, Louis Vuitton, Seize sur Vingt, Dunhill. **Page 102:** Suit by Z Zegna. **Pages 106–107:** From left: Suit by Prada. Coat by Ralph Lauren. Shirt by Prada. Tie by Polo by Ralph Lauren. Tie bar by Burberry London. Belt by Dior Homme. Shoes by Dior Homme. Shirt by Dolce & Gabbana. Tie by Steven Alan. Shirt by Dior Homme by Hedi Slimane. Shoes by Giorgio Armani. Shirt by Jil Sander. Sweater by Jil Sander. Shoes by Marc Jacobs. Knit polo by Prada. Belt by Calvin Klein. Shoes by Adidas. **Page 111:** Suit by Polo by Ralph Lauren. Shirt by Ralph Lauren Black Label. Pocket square by Brooks Brothers. Tie bar by Bulgari. Belt by Valextra.

CHAPTER 6: FORMALWEAR

Pages 116–117: From left: Tuxedo, shirt, and tie by Ralph Laren Purple Label. Shoes by Church's. Tuxedo, shirt, and shoes by Gucci. Cuff links by Jan Leslie. Tuxedo, shirt, and tie by Calvin Klein Collection. Shoes by Allen–Edmonds. Tuxedo by Just Cavalli. Shirt by Tomas Pink. Tie by Brooks Brothers. Shoes by Charles Tyrwhitt. Tuxedo, shirt, and tie by Versace. Shoes by John Lobb. **Pages 118–119:** Tuxedos by Calvin Klein, Charles Nolan, Dolce & Gabbana, Tom Ford for Gucci. **Pages 120–121:** Top row, from left: Shirts by Giorgio Armani, Calvin Klein Collection, Lorenzini, Louis Vuitton. Bottom row, from left: Shoes by Tom Ford for Yves Saint Laurent Rive Gauche, Bally, Gucci. Bow ties by Thomas Pink, Ralph Lauren Purple Label, Best of Class by Robert Talbott, Brioni. Ties by Prada. **Page 124:** Tuxedo, shirt, and shoes by Salvatore Ferragamo. Tie by Polo by Ralph Lauren. Pocket square by Seaward and Searn. **Page 127:** Tuxedo by Dior Homme by Hedi Slimane. Shirt by Boss Selection. Bow tie by Burberry Prorsum. Shoes by Bally.

CHAPTER 7: JEANS

PAGES 132–133: Jeans by Guess, Yves Saint Laurent, A.P.C., DKNY Jeans, Diesel. **Page 134:** Jeans by Levi's. **Pages 134–135:** From left: Jeans by Corpus, Marc Jacobs, Levi's, Diesel, Wrangler by Marc Jacobs. **Page 138:** Jeans by Helmut Lang. Shoes by Asics Onitsuka. **Pages 138–139:** From left: Jeans by Crate. Blazer by Ermenegildo Zegna. Shirt by DKNY. Tie by Theory. Shoes by John Varvatos. Shirt by Penguin. Sweater by Hermès. Tie by Ermenegildo Zegna. Shoes by Dior Homme. Polo shirt by Dior Homme. Belt by John Varvatos. Shoes by Vans. **Page 143:** Shirt by Prada. Tie by Steven Alan. Jeans by Acne Jeans.

CHAPTER 8: CASUAL SHIRTS

Page 148–149: Clockwise from top: Shirts by Pringle of Scotland Red Label, Calvin Klein, Jean Paul Gaultier, Dolce & Gabbana, Diesel, Michael Kors, Y's Yohji Yamamoto. **Pages 152–153:** Top row, from left: Shirts by DKNY, Boss, Polo by Ralph Lauren, Gap, Tommy Hilfiger. Bottom row, from left: Shirts by Polo by Ralph Lauren, Dsquared², Neil Barrett for PUMA, Perry Ellis. **Page 154:** Shirt by Lacoste. **Pages 156–157:** From left: Polo shirt by Lacoste. Blazer by Prada. Jeans by Spurr. Belt by Dior Homme. Shoes by Church's. Jacket by Earnest Sewn. Pants by Bottega Veneta. Belt by John Varvatos. Shoes by

Converse. Pants by Giorgio Armani. Belt by Bobby Jones. Shoes by Sperry Topsider. *Page 159:* Blazer by Brooks Brothers. Shirt by Lacoste. Pants and belt by J. Crew.

CHAPTER 9: SWEATERS

Pages 164–165: Sweater by Gant. Shirt by Band of Outsiders. *Page 168:* Sweater by Tse. *Pages 170–171:* Top row, from left: Sweaters by Prada, A.P.C., Studio Chereskin, Polo by Ralph Lauren, Banana Republic. Bottom row, from left: Sweaters by Acne Jeans, Jil Sander. Cardigan by Le Tigre. Fisherman sweater by Travata. *Page 172:* Sweater and shirt by Gucci. *Pages 174–175:* From left: Sweater by A.P.C. Shirt by Jil Sander. Jean by Corpus. Shoe by A.P.C. Top by Theory. Pants by J. Crew. Sneakers by Common Projects. Sweater by A.P.C. Shirt by Jil Sander. Coat by Acne Jeans. Pants by Prada. Shoes by Johnston & Murphy. Tie by Valentino.

CHAPTER 10: OUTERWEAR

Pages 184–185: Coat by Burberry London. Jacket by Louis Vuitton. Zip–up by PUMA. *Page 188:* Coat by Belvest. *Pages 190–191:* Top row, from left: Coats by Nautica Jeans Company, Coach, Levi's, Kenneth Cole, Barbour. Bottom row, from left: Coats by Dunhill, Coach, Martin Margiela 14, Burberry. Hussein Chalayan, Unis. *Page 192:* Coat by Polo by Ralph Lauren. Sweater by DKNY. Shirt by John Varvatos Star USA. Jeans by ACNE. *Page 195:* Coat by Polo by Ralph Lauren. Shirt by Tom Ford for Gucci. Blazer by Tom Ford for Yves Saint Laurent Rive Gauche. Belt from Search & Destroy. Jeans by Diesel. *Pages 196–197:* From left: Coat by Z Zegna. Turtleneck by Burberry London. Suit by Z Zegna. Shoes by John Varvatos. Gloves by Coach. Scarf by Coach. Hat by Nom De Guerre. Coat by Z Zegna. Shirt by Steven Alan. Jeans by Earnest Sewn. Scarf by John Varvatos for Converse. Shoes by Converse. Jacket by Levi's. Sweater by Theory. Jeans by Earnest Sewn. Belt by DKNY. Scarf by TSE. Shoes by Church's. *Page 199:* Jacket by Louis Vuitton. Shirt by Steven Alan. Tie by Prada.

CHAPTER 11: UNDERWEAR

Pages 204–205: From left: Socks by Nassow, Saks Fifth Avenue, Pantherella. *Page 204:* Top row, from left: Pajamas by Turnbull & Asser. Undershirt by Hanes. Middle row, from left: Briefs and boxers by Calvin Klein. Boxer Briefs by Polo Ralph Lauren. Bottom row, from left: Athletic socks by Gold Toe. Dress Sock by Saks Fifth Avenue.

CHAPTER 12: SHOES

Pages 218–219: Top row, from left: Shoes by Prada, Tods, Boss, Ralph Lauren, Cole Haan. Bottom row, from left: Shoes by Salvatore Ferragamo, Ralph Lauren, Havaianas, Timberland, Tods. *Page 223:* Shoes by Adidas.

CHAPTER 13: ACCESSORIES

Page 235: Top row, from left: Gloves by Yves Saint Laurent. Hat by Gieves. Middle row, from left: Hats by Polo by Ralph Lauren, Chaos, A.P.C. Bottom row, from left: Scarves by Polo by Ralph Lauren, J. Press, Armand Diradourian. *Page 237:* From top: Belts by Louis Vuitton, Cole Haan, Anderson's, Gucci, Energie. *Pages 238:* Portrait: Sunglasses by Stark Eyes. Still Life, from top to bottom: Sunglasses by Jack Spade, Paul Smith, Ermenegildo Zegna, Ray–Ban, Prada Linea Rose, República. *Page 239:* Portrait (top): Sunglasses by Dior Homme by Hedi Slimane. Still Life (top), from top to bottom: Sunglasses by Morgenthal–Frederics, Dolce & Gabbana, Oliver Peoples, Yves Saint Laurent, Burberry, Valentino. Portrait (bottom): Sunglasses by Gucci. Still Life (bottom), from top to bottom: Sunglasses by Dior Homme by Hedi Slimane, Sean John, Persol, Louis Vuitton, Calvin Klein, John Varvatos. *Page 241:* Watch by Rolex. *Pages 242–243:* Top row, from left: Watches by Patek Philippe, Cartier, Casio, Tag Heuer, Versace. Bottom row, from left: Cuff links by Charles Tyrwhitt, Cartier, Brooks Brothers, Hermès. *Page 247:* Top row, from left: Bags by Giorgio Armani, Ralph Lauren. Bottom row, from left: Louis Vuitton, Bobby Jones. *Pages 248–249:* Top row, from left: Bags by Y–3, Jack Spade. Wallets by Comme de Garçons, Hermès. Bottom row, from left: T. Anthony. Dopp kit by Tods. Wallet by Gucci.

Photo and Illustration Credits

All illustrations by Kate Francis.

CONTENTS

Page 4: Charles Masters. *Page 12:* All photos by Jens Mortensen. *Page 13:* All photos by Jens Mortensen, except blue shirt, photo by Jen Campbell.

CHAPTER 1: SHIRTS

Pages 14–15: Jens Mortensen. *Page 18:* Richard Pierce. *Pages 20–21:* All Jens Mortensen, except (top left) Jen Campbell and (bottom left) Andrew McKim. *Page 22:* Eric Ray Davidson. *Page 24:* Jens Mortensen. *Pages 26–27:* Charles Masters, styling by John Olson. *Page 29:* Eric Ray Davidson. *Page 30:* Clockwise from left: John Shearer/WireImage/Newscom, Frank Mullen/WireImage, Granitz/WireImage. *Page 32:* Clockwise from top left: Gary Hersom/Reuters/Newscom, NY3/Zuma Press/Newscom, NY1/Zuma Press/Newscom, LKA/ARB/Wenn/Newscom. *Page 33:* Clockwise from top left: Baxter/ABACA Press/Newscom, Hulton Archive/Getty/Newscom, Jim Ross/Getty Images, Kathy Hutchins/Zuma Press/Newscom, RH5/ZOB/Wenn Photos/Newscom.

CHAPTER 2: PANTS

Pages 34–35: Luke Irons. *Page 38:* Jens Mortensen, styling by Solange Sandstrom. *Pages 40–43:* Jens Mortensen, styling by Bettina Budewig. *Page 44:* Greg Broom. *Page 46:* David Black. *Pages 48:* Jens Mortensen. *Page 49:* Top row: Jens Mortensen. Bottom row: Mike Lorrig. *Pages 50–51:* Charles Masters, styling by John Olson. *Page 53:* Carlton Davis. *Page 54:* Left: Frazer Harrison/Getty Images for Sony. Right: Granitz/WireImage. *Page 56:* Photo courtesy of Giorgio Armani.

CHAPTER 3: BLAZERS

Pages 58–59: Eric Ray Davidson. *Page 62:* Jens Mortensen. *Pages 64–65:* Jens Mortensen, except (bottom left) Mike Lorrig. *Page 66:* Peter Stanglmayr. *Pages 68–69:* Charles Masters, styling by John Olson. *Page 71:* Brooke Nipar. *Page 72:* Clockwise from left: Bryan Bedder/Getty Images, M. Sullivan/WireImage, Phillips/WireImage.

CHAPTER 4: TIES

Pages 76–77: Richard Pierce. *Pages 78–79:* Jens Mortensen, except (top left) Andrew McKim. *Page 80:* Randall Mesdon. *Page 84:* Top: John Slater/Corbis. Bottom: French School/Bridgeman Art Library/Getty Images. *Page 85:* Top row: Fred Prouser/Reuters/Newscom, Caulfield/WireImage. Bottom row, from left: Time & Life Pictures/Getty Images, ABC/Courtesy Everett Collection. *Pages 86–87:* Greg Broom. *Page 86:* Clockwise from left: Bravo/Photofest, Evan Agostini/Getty Images, Richard Lewis/WireImage. *Page 90:* Dean Kaufman.

CHAPTER 5: SUITS

Pages 92–93: Eric Ray Davidson. *Page 96:* Jens Mortensen. *Pages 98–101:* Jens Mortensen, styling by Bettina Budewig. *Page 102:* Randall Mesdon. *Pages 106–107:* Charles Masters, styling by John Olson. *Page 108:* Top row, from left: Hulton-Deutsch Collection/Corbis, courtesy Everett Collection. Bottom row, from left: courtesy Everett Collection, 20th Century Fox/courtesy Everett Collection, courtesy Everett Collection. *Page 109:* Top row, from left: Universal TV/courtesy Everett Collection, James Devaney/WireImage. Bottom row, from left: 20th Century Fox/courtesy Everett Collection, Jeffrey Mayer/WireImage. *Page 111:* James Macari. *Page 112:* Left: K. Olsen/WireImage. Right: Kevin Mazur/WireImage.

CHAPTER 6: FORMALWEAR

Pages 116–117: Daniel Gabbay. *Pages 120–123:* Jens Mortensen. *Page 124:* Daniel Gabbay. *Page 127:* Eric Ray Davidson. *Page 128:* Left: Celebrity Vibe/Bauer-Griffin.com. Right: Granitz/WireImage. *Page 130:* Gillian Lamb.

CHAPTER 7: JEANS

Pages 132–133: Kira Bunse. *Page 134:* Greg Broom. *Pages 136–137:* Jens Mortensen, styling by Bettina Budewig. *Page 138:* Ben Grieme. *Pages 140–141:* Charles Masters, styling by John Olson. *Page 143:* Greg Broom. *Page 144:* Left: S. Lovekin/WireImage. Right: Matrix/Bauer-Griffin.com. *Page 146:* Photo by Dean Kaufman.

CHAPTER 8: CASUAL SHIRTS

Pages 148–149: Charles Masters. *Pages 152–153:* Jens Mortensen. *Page 154:* Jen Campbell. *Pages 156–157:* Charles Masters, styling by John Olson. *Page 159:* Jen Campbell. *Page 160:* Left: Spellman/WireImage. Right: Marcel Hartmann/Corbis. *Page 162:* Rebecca Greenfield.

CHAPTER 9: SWEATERS

Pages 164–165: Andrew Burmeister. *Page 168:* Jens Mortensen. *Page 170:* Jens Mortensen, except (bottom right) Greg Broom. *Page 171:* Top row, all Jens Mortensen, (bottom left) Jens Mortensen, (bottom middle) Plamen Petkev, (bottom right) Greg Broom. *Page 172:* Luke Irons. *Pages 174–175:* Charles Masters, styling John Olson. *Page 177:* Peter Stanglmayr. *Page 178:* Left: Ron Galella/WireImage. Right: Handout/MCT/Newscom. *Page 180–181:* All photos courtesy of Everett Collection, except *Thomas Crown Affair* © Beitia Archives/Digital Press/Newscom, *Rebel Without A Cause*, photo courtesy of Keystone/Getty Hulton Archive/Newscom. *Pages 182:* Photo courtesy of Burberry.

CHAPTER 10: OUTERWEAR

Pages 184–185: Eric Ray Davidson. *Page 188:* Greg Broom. *Page 190:* Jens Mortensen. *Page 191:* Jens Mortensen, except (top middle) Plamen Petkov, (bottom middle) Mike Lorrig. *Page 192:* Carlotta Manaigo. *Page 195:* Ben Grieme. *Pages 196–197:* Charles Masters, styling by John Olson. *Page 199:* Andy Eaton. *Page 200:* Left: Steven Henry/Stringer/Getty Images. Right: David E. Brown. *Page 202:* David Black.

CHAPTER 11: UNDERWEAR

Pages 204–205: Jens Mortensen, styling by Solange Sandstrom. *Page 206:* Jens Mortensen, styling by Solange Sandstrom, except for pajamas. *Page 209:* Jen Campbell. *Page 210:* Left: Mazur/WireImage. Right: Jason Merritt/FilmMagic.com. *Page 212:* Juliana Sohn.

CHAPTER 12: SHOES

Pages 214–215: Charles Masters. *Page 218:* Jens Mortensen, except (bottom right) Norman Schwartz. *Page 219:* Jens Mortensen, except (bottom left) Mike Lorrig. *Page 220:* Jens Mortensen, styling by Solange Sandstrom. *Page 223:* Greg Broom. *Page 224:* Left: Mario Tama/Getty Images. Right Bettmann/Corbis. *Page 225:* Top row, from left: Universal/courtesy the Everett Collection, NY Photo Press/Photographer Showcase/Newscom, Ray Tamarra/Getty Images. Bottom row: Hulton Archive/Newscom. *Page 227:* Vincent Dilio. *Page 228:* Left: Patrick Riviere/Getty Images. Right: Rebecca Greenfield. *Page 230:* Photo courtesy of Versace.

CHAPTER 13: ACCESSORIES

Pages 232–233: Mike Lorrig. *Pages 235:* Jens Mortensen, styling by Solange Sandstrom. *Page 237:* Jens Mortensen, except (bottom) Richard Pierce. *Pages 238–239:* Portraits by KT Auleta. Still Lifes by Greg Broom. *Page 241:* Greg Broom. *Pages 242–243:* Jens Mortensen, except (top, second from left) Robin Broadbent. *Page 245:* Jeffrey Cohen. *Page 247:* Top row: Charles Masters, Jens Mortensen. Bottom row: Jens Mortensen, Charles Masters. *Page 248:* Jens Mortensen, except (top right) Jack Spade Co. *Page 249:* Jens Mortensen, except (top left) Chris Gentile.

Penguin Group (Canada) 90 Eglinton Avenue East, Suite 700, Tornoto, Ontario M4P 2Y3, Canada (a division of Pearson Penguin Canada Inc.); Penguin Books Ltd, 80 Strand, London WC2R ORL, England; Penguin Ireland, 25 St Stephen's Green, Dublin 2, Ireland (a division of Penguin Books Ltd); Penguin Group (Australia), 250 Camberwell Road, Camberwell, Victoria 3124, Australia (a division of Pearson Australia Group Pty Ltd); Penguin Books India Pvt Ltd, 11 Community Centre, Panchsheel Park, New Delhi – 110 017, India; Penguin Group (NZ), cnr Airborne and Rosedale Roads, Albany, Auckland 1310, New Zealand (a division of Pearson New Zealand Ltd); Penguin Books (South Africa) (Pty) Ltd, 24 Sturdee Avenue, Rosebank, Johannesburg 2196, South Africa

Penguin Books Ltd, Register Offices:
80 Strand, London WC2R ORL, England

Published by Gotham Books, a Member of Penguin Group (USA) Inc.

First Printing, October 2007

10 9 8 7 6 5 4

Gotham Books and the skyscraper logo are trademarks of Penguin Group (USA) Inc.

ISBN 978-1-592-40328-8

Printed in China